www.EffortlessMath.com

... So Much More Online!

✓ FREE Math lessons

✓ More Math learning books!

✓ Mathematics Worksheets

✓ Online Math Tutors

Need a PDF version of this book?

Send email to: Info@EffortlessMath.com

FSA 8 Math Prep 2019 – 2020

Step-By-Step FSA 8 Math Study Guide

By

Reza Nazari

& Sam Mest

All inquiries should be addressed to:

info@effortlessMath.com

www.EffortlessMath.com

ISBN–13: 978-1-64612-051-2

ISBN–10: 1-64612-051-5

Published by: Effortless Math Education

www.EffortlessMath.com

Description

FSA 8 Math Prep 2019 – 2020, which reflects the 2019 - 2020 test guidelines, provides students with the confidence and math skills they need to succeed on the FSA 8 Math test. It is designed to address the needs of FSA 8 test takers who must have a working knowledge of basic Math. The step-by-step guide and hundreds of examples in this book help you improve your math skills and raise your FSA 8 Math scores.

Two full-length FSA 8 Math tests with detailed answers and explanations can help you discover your weak areas for concentrated study. Here is a valuable learning tool for the FSA 8 test takers who need to improve their knowledge of Mathematics and prepare for the FSA 8 Math test. After completing this workbook, you will have solid foundation and adequate practice that is necessary to ace the FSA 8 Math test.

FSA 8 Math Prep 2019 – 2020 contains many exciting features to help you ace the FSA 8 Math test, including:

- Content 100% aligned with the 2019 FSA 8 test
- Prepared by FSA 8 Math experts
- Complete coverage of all FSA 8 Math topics which you will need to ace the test
- Step-by-step guide for all FSA 8 Math topics
- Topics are grouped by category, so you can easily focus on the topics you struggle on
- 2 complete FSA 8 Math practice tests (featuring new question types) with detailed answers

FSA 8 Math Prep 2019 – 2020 is an incredibly useful tool for those FSA 8 test takers who want to review core content areas, brush-up in math, discover their strengths and weaknesses, and achieve their best scores on the FSA 8 test.

The only prep book you will ever need to succeed on the FSA 8 Math Test!

Contents

Chapter 1:
Whole Numbers

Math Topics that you'll learn today:

- ✓ Rounding
- ✓ Whole Number Addition and Subtraction
- ✓ Whole Number Multiplication and Division
- ✓ Rounding and Estimates

Rounding

Step-by-step guide:

Rounding is putting a number up or down to the nearest whole number or the nearest hundred, etc.

- ✓ *First, find the place value you'll round to.*
- ✓ *Find the digit to the right of the place value you're rounding to. If it is 5 or bigger, add 1 to the place value you're rounding to and put zero for all digits on its right side. If the digit to the right of the place value is less than 5, keep the place value and put zero for all digits to the right.*

Examples:

1) Round 83 to the nearest ten.

The place value of ten is 8. The digit on the right side is 3 (which is less than 5). Keep 8 and put zero for the digit on the right side. The answer is 80. 83 rounded to the nearest ten is 80, because 83 is closer to 80 than to 90.

2) Round 554 to the nearest hundred.

554 rounded to the nearest hundred is 600, because the digits on the right side of hundred place is 54. Add 1 to 5 and put zeros for other digits. The answer is 600.

✍ *Round each number to the nearest ten.*

1) 98 = ____   4) 18 = ____
2) 86 = ____   5) 47 = ____
3) 21 = ____   6) 61 = ____

✍ *Round each number to the nearest hundred.*

7) 121 = ____   10) 729 = ____
8) 149 = ____   11) 591 = ____
9) 836 = ____   12) 382 = ____

Whole Number Addition and Subtraction

Step-by-step guide:

- ✓ *Line up the numbers.*
- ✓ *Start with the unit place. (ones place)*
- ✓ *Regroup if necessary.*
- ✓ *Add or subtract the tens place.*
- ✓ *Continue with other digits.*

Examples:

1) Find the sum. $364 + 256 = ?$

First line up the numbers: $\begin{array}{r} 364 \\ +256 \\ \hline \end{array}$ → Start with the unit place. (ones place) $6 + 4 = 10$,

Write 0 for ones place and keep 1, $\begin{array}{r} 1 \\ 364 \\ +256 \\ \hline 0 \end{array}$, Add the tens place and the digit 1 we kept:

$1 + 6 + 5 = 12$, Write 2 and keep 1, $\begin{array}{r} 1\,1 \\ 364 \\ +256 \\ \hline 20 \end{array}$

Continue with other digits → $1 + 2 + 3 = 6$ → $\begin{array}{r} 1\,1 \\ 264 \\ +256 \\ \hline 620 \end{array}$

2) Find the difference. $756 - 435 = ?$

First line up the numbers: $\begin{array}{r} 756 \\ -435 \\ \hline \end{array}$, → Start with the unit place. $6 - 5 = 1$, $\begin{array}{r} 756 \\ -435 \\ \hline 1 \end{array}$,

Subtract the tens place. $5 - 3 = 2$, $\begin{array}{r} 756 \\ -435 \\ \hline 21 \end{array}$, Continue with other digits → $7 - 4 = 3$, $\begin{array}{r} 756 \\ -435 \\ \hline 321 \end{array}$

✎ *Find the sum or difference.*

1) $3,529 + 746 =$

2) $1,921 - 836 =$

3) $2,922 - 1,820 =$

4) $2,003 + 564 =$

5) $1,702 - 951 =$

6) $4,202 - 3,985 =$

7) $932 + 1,123 =$

8) $1,136 + 2,009 =$

Whole Number Multiplication

Step-by-step guide:

- ✓ Learn the times tables first! To solve multiplication problems fast, you need to memorize the times table. For example, 5 times 7 is 35 or 9 times 6 is 54.
- ✓ For multiplication, line up the numbers you are multiplying.
- ✓ Start with the ones place and regroup if necessary.
- ✓ Continue with other digits.

Examples:

1) Solve. $215 \times 20 = ?$

Line up the numbers: $\begin{array}{r} 215 \\ \times\ 20 \\ \hline \end{array}$, start with the ones place → $0 \times 215 = 0$, $\begin{array}{r} 215 \\ \times\ 20 \\ \hline 0 \end{array}$, Continue

with other digit which is 2. → $215 \times 2 = 430$, $\begin{array}{r} 215 \\ \times\ 20 \\ \hline 4{,}300 \end{array}$

2) Solve. $421 \times 18 = ?$

Line up the numbers: $\begin{array}{r} 421 \\ \times\ 18 \\ \hline \end{array}$, start with the ones place → $8 \times 1 = 8$, $\begin{array}{r} 421 \\ \times\ 18 \\ \hline 8 \end{array}$, $8 \times 2 = 16$,

write 6 and keep 1. $\begin{array}{r} 421 \\ \times\ 18 \\ \hline 68 \end{array}$, → $8 \times 4 = 32$, add 1 to 32, the answer is 33. $\begin{array}{r} 421 \\ \times\ 18 \\ \hline 3{,}368 \end{array}$

Now, write 0 in the next line and multiply 421 by 1, using the same process. (Since 1 is in the tens place, we need to write 0 before doing the operation). The answer is 4210.
Add 4,210 and 3,368. The answer is: $4{,}210 + 3{,}368 = 7{,}578$

🖎 *Find the missing number.*

1) $36 \times 9 =$ _____
2) $17 \times 5 =$ _____
3) $195 \times 10 =$ _____
4) $422 \times 15 =$ _____

5) $231 \times 29 =$ _____
6) $105 \times 17 =$ _____
7) $612 \times 11 =$ _____
8) $191 \times 24 =$ _____

Whole Number Division

Step-by-step guide:

Division: A typical division problem: Dividend ÷ Divisor = Quotient

- In division, we want to find how many times a number (divisor) is contained in another number (dividend). The result in a division problem is the quotient.
- ✓ First, write the problem in division format. (dividend is inside; divisor is outside)

$$\text{Divisor} \,\overline{)\,\text{Dividend}}^{\text{Quotient}}$$

- ✓ Now, find how many times divisor goes into dividend. (if it is a big number, break the dividend into smaller numbers by choosing the appropriate number of digits from left. Start from the first digit on the left side of the divided and see if the divisor will go into it. If not, keep moving over one digit to the right in the dividend until you have a number the divisor will go into.
- ✓ Find number of times the divisor goes into the part of the dividend you chose.
- ✓ Write the answer above the digit in the dividend you are using and multiply it by the divisor and Write the product under the part of the dividend you are using, then subtract.
- ✓ Bring down the next digit in the dividend and repeat this process until you have nothing

    left to bring down.

Example: Solve. $516 \div 8 = ?$

- ✓ First, write the problem in division format. $8\,\overline{)\,516}$
- ✓ Start from left digit of the dividend. 8 doesn't go into 5. So, choose another digit of the dividend. It is 1.
- ✓ Now, find how many times 8 goes into 51. The answer is 6. $8\,\overline{)\,516}^{\;6}$
- ✓ Write 6 above the dividend part. 8 times 6 is 48. Write 48 below 51 and subtract. The answer is 3.
- ✓ Now bring down the next digit which is 6. How many times 8 goes into 36? The answer is 4. Write 4 above dividend. This is the final step since there is no other digit of the dividend to bring down. The final answer is 64 and the remainder is 4.

$$\begin{array}{r} 64 \\ 8\,\overline{)\,516} \\ -48 \\ \hline 36 \\ -32 \\ \hline 4 \end{array}$$

✎ Solve.

1) $244 \div 8 =$ _____

2) $156 \div 7 =$ _____

3) $622 \div 6 =$ _____

4) $208 \div 9 =$ _____

5) $428 \div 12 =$ _____

6) $612 \div 14 =$ _____

7) $585 \div 13 =$ _____

8) $875 \div 25 =$ _____

Rounding and Estimates

Step-by-step guide:

Rounding and estimating are math strategies used for approximating a number. To estimate means to make a rough guess or calculation. To round means to simplify a known number by scaling it slightly up or down.

✓ To estimate a math operation, round the numbers.
✓ For 2-digit numbers, your usually can round to the nearest tens, for 3-digit numbers, round to nearest hundreds, etc.
✓ Find the answer.

Examples:

1) Estimate the sum by rounding each number to the nearest hundred. $256 + 145 =?$
256 rounded to the nearest hundred is 300. 145 rounded to the nearest hundred is 100.
Then: $300 + 100 = 400$

2) Estimate the result by rounding each number to the nearest ten. $84 - 66 = ?$
84 rounded to the nearest ten is 80. 66 rounded to the nearest ten is 70.
Then: $80 - 70 = 10$

✍ *Estimate the sum by rounding each number to the nearest ten.*

1) $17 + 44 =$ _____   4) $62 + 71 =$ _____

2) $94 + 67 =$ _____   5) $462 + 751 =$ _____

3) $44 + 28 =$ _____   6) $837 + 555 =$ _____

✍ *Estimate the product by rounding each number to the nearest ten.*

7) $27 \times 18 =$ _____   10) $39 \times 52 =$ _____

8) $33 \times 29 =$ _____   11) $46 \times 72 =$ _____

9) $72 \times 14 =$ _____   12) $91 \times 32 =$ _____

Answers

Rounding

1) 100
2) 90
3) 20
4) 20

5) 50
6) 60
7) 100
8) 100

9) 800
10) 700
11) 600
12) 400

Whole Number Addition and Subtraction

1) 4,275
2) 1,085
3) 1,102

4) 2,567
5) 751
6) 217

7) 2,055
8) 3,145

Whole Number Multiplication

1) 324
2) 85
3) 1,950

4) 6,330
5) 6,699
6) 1,785

7) 6,732
8) 4,584

Whole Number Division

1) $30, r4$
2) $22, r2$
3) $103, r4$

4) $23, r1$
5) $35, r8$
6) $43, r10$

7) 45
8) 35

Rounding and Estimates

1) 60
2) 160
3) 70
4) 130

5) 1,300
6) 1,400
7) 600
8) 900

9) 700
10) 2,000
11) 3,500
12) 2,700

Chapter 2: Fractions

Math Topics that you'll learn today:

- ✓ Comparing Numbers

- ✓ Simplifying Fractions

- ✓ Adding and Subtracting Fractions

- ✓ Multiplying and Dividing Fractions

Simplifying Fractions

Step-by-step guide:

✓ Evenly divide both the top and bottom of the fraction by $2, 3, 5, 7, \dots$ etc.

✓ Continue until you can't go any further.

Examples:

1) Simplify $\frac{18}{54}$.

To simplify $\frac{18}{54}$, find a number that both 18 and 54 are divisible by. Both are divisible by 18.

Then: $\frac{18}{54} = \frac{18 \div 18}{54 \div 18} = \frac{1}{3}$

2) Simplify $\frac{50}{125}$.

To simplify $\frac{50}{125}$, find a number that both 50 and 125 are divisible by. Both are divisible by 5 and 25. Then: $\frac{50}{125} = \frac{50 \div 5}{125 \div 5} = \frac{10}{25}$, 10 and 25 are divisible by 5, then: $\frac{10}{25} = \frac{2}{5}$

or $\frac{50}{125} = \frac{50 \div 25}{125 \div 25} = \frac{2}{5}$

✍ *Simplify each fraction.*

1) $\frac{18}{42} =$

2) $\frac{12}{66} =$

3) $\frac{15}{45} =$

4) $\frac{9}{24} =$

5) $\frac{26}{117} =$

6) $\frac{14}{77} =$

7) $\frac{16}{80} =$

8) $\frac{20}{50} =$

9) $\frac{34}{153} =$

10) $\frac{33}{60} =$

11) $\frac{15}{70} =$

12) $\frac{27}{63} =$

Adding and Subtracting Fractions

Step-by-step guide:

- ✓ For "like" fractions (fractions with the same denominator), add or subtract the numerators and write the answer over the common denominator.
- ✓ Find equivalent fractions with the same denominator before you can add or subtract fractions with different denominators.
- ✓ Adding and Subtracting with the same denominator:

$$\frac{a}{b} + \frac{c}{b} = \frac{a+c}{b} \quad , \quad \frac{a}{b} - \frac{c}{b} = \frac{a-c}{b}$$

- ✓ Adding and Subtracting fractions with different denominators:

$$\frac{a}{b} + \frac{c}{d} = \frac{ad+cb}{bd} \quad , \quad \frac{a}{b} - \frac{c}{d} = \frac{ad-cb}{bd}$$

Examples:

1) Subtract fractions. $\frac{6}{9} - \frac{2}{9} =$

For "like" fractions, subtract the numerators and write the answer over the common denominator. then: $\frac{6}{9} - \frac{2}{9} = \frac{4}{9}$

2) Subtract fractions. $\frac{5}{8} - \frac{2}{5} =$

For "unlike" fractions, find equivalent fractions with the same denominator before you can add or subtract fractions with different denominators. Use this formula: $\frac{a}{b} - \frac{c}{d} = \frac{ad-cb}{bd}$

$\frac{5}{8} - \frac{2}{5} = \frac{(5)(5) - (2)(8)}{8 \times 5} = \frac{25-16}{40} = \frac{9}{40}$

✏️ *Find the sum or difference.*

1) $\frac{2}{5} + \frac{4}{5} =$

2) $\frac{3}{4} + \frac{1}{4} =$

3) $\frac{2}{7} + \frac{4}{7} =$

4) $\frac{1}{2} + \frac{3}{5} =$

5) $\frac{4}{9} - \frac{1}{4} =$

6) $\frac{7}{8} - \frac{2}{3} =$

7) $\frac{5}{8} - \frac{1}{2} =$

8) $\frac{9}{10} - \frac{5}{8} =$

9) $\frac{7}{12} - \frac{2}{7} =$

Multiplying and Dividing Fractions

Step-by-step guide:

- ✓ Multiplying fractions: multiply the top numbers and multiply the bottom numbers.
- ✓ Dividing fractions: Keep, Change, Flip
- ✓ Keep first fraction, change division sign to multiplication, and flip the numerator and denominator of the second fraction. Then, solve!

Examples:

1) Multiplying fractions. $\frac{4}{7} \times \frac{3}{8} =$

Multiply the top numbers and multiply the bottom numbers.

$\frac{4}{7} \times \frac{3}{8} = \frac{4 \times 3}{7 \times 8} = \frac{12}{56}$, simplify: $\frac{12}{56} = \frac{12 \div 4}{56 \div 4} = \frac{3}{14}$

2) Dividing fractions. $\frac{2}{3} \div \frac{1}{5} =$

Keep first fraction, change division sign to multiplication, and flip the numerator and denominator of the second fraction. Then: $\frac{2}{3} \times \frac{5}{1} = \frac{2 \times 5}{3 \times 1} = \frac{10}{3}$

✍ *Find the answers.*

1) $\frac{2}{5} \times \frac{3}{4} =$

2) $\frac{7}{10} \times \frac{1}{2} =$

3) $\frac{2}{7} \times \frac{4}{5} =$

4) $\frac{3}{8} \times \frac{2}{9} =$

5) $\frac{4}{6} \times \frac{8}{9} =$

6) $\frac{6}{7} \times \frac{2}{3} =$

7) $\frac{2}{3} \div \frac{1}{8} =$

8) $\frac{3}{5} \div \frac{2}{5} =$

9) $\frac{5}{9} \div \frac{1}{6} =$

10) $\frac{3}{8} \div \frac{3}{4} =$

11) $\frac{5}{9} \div \frac{10}{12} =$

12) $\frac{6}{10} \div \frac{4}{5} =$

Answers

Simplifying Fractions

1) $\dfrac{3}{7}$

2) $\dfrac{2}{11}$

3) $\dfrac{1}{3}$

4) $\dfrac{3}{8}$

5) $\dfrac{2}{9}$

6) $\dfrac{2}{11}$

7) $\dfrac{1}{5}$

8) $\dfrac{2}{5}$

9) $\dfrac{2}{9}$

10) $\dfrac{11}{20}$

11) $\dfrac{3}{14}$

12) $\dfrac{3}{7}$

Adding and Subtracting Fractions

1) $\dfrac{6}{5}$

2) $\dfrac{4}{4} = 1$

3) $\dfrac{6}{7}$

4) $\dfrac{11}{10}$

5) $\dfrac{7}{36}$

6) $\dfrac{5}{24}$

7) $\dfrac{2}{16} = \dfrac{1}{8}$

8) $\dfrac{22}{80} = \dfrac{11}{40}$

9) $\dfrac{25}{84}$

Multiplying and Dividing Fractions

1) $\dfrac{3}{10}$

2) $\dfrac{7}{20}$

3) $\dfrac{8}{35}$

4) $\dfrac{1}{12}$

5) $\dfrac{16}{27}$

6) $\dfrac{4}{7}$

7) $\dfrac{16}{3}$

8) $\dfrac{3}{2}$

9) $\dfrac{10}{3}$

10) $\dfrac{1}{2}$

11) $\dfrac{2}{3}$

12) $\dfrac{3}{4}$

Chapter 3: Mixed Numbers

Math Topics that you'll learn today:

- ✓ Adding Mixed Numbers

- ✓ Subtracting Mixed Numbers

- ✓ Multiplying Mixed Numbers

- ✓ Dividing Mixed Numbers

Adding Mixed Numbers

Step-by-step guide:

Use the following steps for both adding and subtracting mixed numbers.

- ✓ Add whole numbers of the mixed numbers.
- ✓ Add the fractions of each mixed number.
- ✓ Find the Least Common Denominator (LCD) if necessary.
- ✓ Add whole numbers and fractions.
- ✓ Write your answer in lowest terms.

Examples:

1) Add mixed numbers. $2\frac{2}{5} + 1\frac{3}{7} =$

Rewriting our equation with parts separated, $2 + \frac{2}{5} + 1 + \frac{3}{7}$, Solving the whole number parts $1 + 2 = 3$, Solving the fraction parts $\frac{2}{5} + \frac{3}{7}$, and rewrite to solve with the equivalent fractions.

$\frac{14}{35} + \frac{15}{35} = \frac{29}{35}$, then Combining the whole and fraction parts $3 + \frac{29}{35} = 3\frac{29}{35}$

2) Add mixed numbers. $3\frac{1}{2} + 2\frac{3}{4} =$

Rewriting our equation with parts separated, $3 + \frac{1}{2} + 2 + \frac{3}{4}$, Solving the whole number parts $3 + 2 = 5$, Solving the fraction parts $\frac{1}{2} + \frac{3}{4}$, and rewrite to solve with the equivalent fractions.

$\frac{2}{4} + \frac{3}{5} = \frac{5}{4} = 1\frac{1}{4}$, then Combining the whole and fraction parts $5 + 1 + \frac{1}{4} = 6\frac{1}{4}$

✍ *Find the sum.*

1) $5\frac{2}{5} + 3\frac{3}{10} =$

2) $2\frac{2}{3} + 2\frac{5}{9} =$

3) $1\frac{4}{7} + 2\frac{2}{3} =$

4) $3\frac{2}{5} + 3\frac{1}{2} =$

5) $5\frac{3}{4} + 3\frac{1}{8} =$

6) $4\frac{2}{9} + 6\frac{4}{5} =$

7) $7\frac{3}{8} + 1\frac{1}{2} =$

8) $2\frac{5}{6} + 7\frac{2}{3} =$

9) $3\frac{4}{5} + 3\frac{4}{7} =$

Subtract Mixed Numbers

Step-by-step guide:

Use the following steps for both adding and subtracting mixed numbers.

- ✓ Subtract the whole number of second mixed number from whole number of the first mixed number.
- ✓ Subtract the second fraction from the first one.
- ✓ Find the Least Common Denominator (LCD) if necessary.
- ✓ Add the result of whole numbers and fractions.
- ✓ Write your answer in lowest terms.

Examples:

1) Subtract. $4\frac{3}{4} - 2\frac{3}{5} =$

Rewriting our equation with parts separated, $4 + \frac{3}{4} - 2 - \frac{3}{5}$

Solving the whole number parts $4 - 2 = 2$, Solving the fraction parts, $\frac{3}{4} - \frac{3}{5} = \frac{15-12}{20} =$ $\frac{3}{20}$. Combining the whole and fraction parts, $2 + \frac{3}{20} = 2\frac{3}{20}$

2) Subtract. $7\frac{5}{8} - 5\frac{1}{3} =$

Rewriting our equation with parts separated, $7 + \frac{5}{8} - 5 - \frac{1}{3}$

Solving the whole number parts $7 - 5 = 2$, Solving the fraction parts, $\frac{5}{8} - \frac{1}{3} = \frac{15-8}{24} = \frac{7}{24}$

Combining the whole and fraction parts, $2 + \frac{7}{24} = 2\frac{7}{24}$

✎ *Find the difference.*

1) $5\frac{3}{4} - 1\frac{7}{9} =$

2) $7\frac{1}{5} - 4\frac{3}{7} =$

3) $4\frac{1}{2} - 3\frac{1}{6} =$

4) $8\frac{4}{5} - 2\frac{3}{4} =$

5) $9\frac{1}{4} - 1\frac{4}{9} =$

6) $3\frac{1}{2} - 1\frac{1}{8} =$

7) $10\frac{3}{8} - 8\frac{1}{9} =$

8) $11\frac{7}{9} - 5\frac{1}{4} =$

9) $15\frac{2}{5} - 7\frac{5}{7} =$

Multiplying Mixed Numbers

Step-by-step guide:

- ✓ Convert the mixed numbers to improper fractions. (improper fraction is a fraction in which the top number is bigger than bottom number)
- ✓ Multiply fractions and simplify if necessary.

$$a\frac{c}{b} = a + \frac{c}{b} = \frac{ab + c}{b}$$

Examples:

1) Multiply mixed numbers. $4\frac{1}{5} \times 1\frac{5}{8} =$

   Converting mixed numbers to fractions, $4\frac{1}{5} = \frac{21}{5}$ and $1\frac{5}{8} = \frac{13}{8}$.

   $\frac{21}{5} \times \frac{13}{8}$, Applying the fractions formula for multiplication, $\frac{21 \times 13}{5 \times 8} = \frac{273}{40} = 6\frac{33}{40}$

2) Multiply mixed numbers. $7\frac{1}{3} \times 3\frac{2}{5} =$

   Converting mixed numbers to fractions, $\frac{22}{3} \times \frac{17}{5}$, Applying the fractions formula for multiplication, $\frac{22 \times 17}{3 \times 5} = \frac{374}{15} = 24\frac{14}{15}$

✍ *Find the product.*

1) $2\frac{2}{7} \times 3\frac{1}{2} =$

2) $4\frac{3}{4} \times 2\frac{3}{8} =$

3) $4\frac{2}{3} \times 3\frac{1}{9} =$

4) $6\frac{1}{6} \times 2\frac{3}{8} =$

5) $2\frac{1}{8} \times 2\frac{5}{6} =$

6) $4\frac{1}{10} \times 3\frac{1}{5} =$

7) $6\frac{5}{7} \times 2\frac{4}{7} =$

8) $5\frac{1}{9} \times 5\frac{2}{7} =$

9) $1\frac{8}{9} \times 2\frac{1}{3} =$

10) $4\frac{6}{8} \times 2\frac{7}{8} =$

Dividing Mixed Numbers

Step-by-step guide:

✓ Convert the mixed numbers to improper fractions.

✓ Divide fractions and simplify if necessary.

$$a\frac{c}{b} = a + \frac{c}{b} = \frac{ab+c}{b}$$

Examples:

1) Find the quotient. $3\frac{3}{8} \div 2\frac{1}{4} =$

Converting mixed numbers to fractions, $\frac{27}{8} \div \frac{9}{4}$, Applying the fractions formula for multiplication, $\frac{27\times4}{8\times9} = \frac{108}{72} = 1\frac{1}{2}$

2) Find the quotient. $5\frac{1}{6} \div 7\frac{5}{9} =$

Converting mixed numbers to fractions, $\frac{31}{6} \div \frac{68}{9}$, Applying the fractions formula for multiplication, $\frac{31\times9}{6\times68} = \frac{279}{408} = \frac{93}{136}$

✍ *Find the quotient.*

1) $5\frac{4}{7} \div 2\frac{2}{5} =$

2) $6\frac{7}{8} \div 2\frac{3}{4} =$

3) $8\frac{2}{3} \div 5\frac{1}{5} =$

4) $6\frac{3}{4} \div 2\frac{5}{8} =$

5) $8\frac{5}{9} \div 3\frac{7}{8} =$

6) $7\frac{1}{7} \div 3\frac{4}{8} =$

7) $9\frac{1}{10} \div 4\frac{4}{5} =$

8) $5\frac{3}{7} \div 4\frac{1}{2} =$

9) $7\frac{1}{2} \div 3\frac{4}{9} =$

10) $10\frac{1}{3} \div 5\frac{4}{9} =$

Answers

Adding Mixed Numbers

1) $8\frac{7}{10}$

2) $5\frac{2}{9}$

3) $4\frac{5}{21}$

4) $6\frac{9}{10}$

5) $8\frac{7}{8}$

6) $11\frac{1}{45}$

7) $8\frac{7}{8}$

8) $10\frac{1}{2}$

9) $7\frac{13}{35}$

Subtract Mixed Numbers

1) $3\frac{35}{36}$

2) $2\frac{27}{35}$

3) $1\frac{1}{3}$

4) $6\frac{1}{20}$

5) $7\frac{29}{36}$

6) $2\frac{3}{8}$

7) $2\frac{19}{72}$

8) $6\frac{19}{36}$

9) $7\frac{24}{35}$

Multiplying Mixed Numbers

1) 8

2) $11\frac{9}{32}$

3) $14\frac{14}{27}$

4) $14\frac{31}{48}$

5) $6\frac{1}{48}$

6) $13\frac{3}{25}$

7) $17\frac{13}{49}$

8) $27\frac{1}{63}$

9) $4\frac{11}{27}$

10) $13\frac{21}{32}$

Dividing Mixed Numbers

1) $2\frac{9}{28}$

2) $2\frac{1}{2}$

3) $1\frac{2}{3}$

4) $2\frac{4}{7}$

5) $2\frac{58}{279}$

6) $2\frac{2}{49}$

7) $1\frac{43}{48}$

8) $1\frac{13}{63}$

9) $2\frac{11}{62}$

10) $1\frac{44}{49}$

Chapter 4: Decimals

Math Topics that you'll learn today:

- ✓ Comparing Decimals

- ✓ Rounding Decimals

- ✓ Adding and Subtracting Decimals

- ✓ Multiplying and Dividing Decimals

Comparing Decimals

Step-by-step guide:

Decimals: is a fraction written in a special form. For example, instead of writing $\frac{1}{5}$ you can write **02**.

For comparing decimals:

✓ Compare each digit of two decimals in the same place value.
✓ Start from left. Compare hundreds, tens, ones, tenth, hundredth, etc.
✓ To compare numbers, use these symbols:
- Equal to =,   Less than <,   Greater than >
  Greater than or equal ≥,   Less than or equal ≤

Examples:

1) Compare 0.30 and 0.13.

   0.30 *is greater than* 0.03, because the tenth place of 0.30 is 3, but the tenth place of 0.03 is one. Then: 0.30 > 0.13

2) Compare 0.0405 and 0.101.

   0.101 *is greater than* 0.0405, because the tenth place of 0.101 is 1, but the tenth place of 0.0405 is zero. Then: 0.0405 < 0.101

✎ *Write the correct comparison symbol (>, < or =).*

1) 0.71 ☐ 0.071

2) 0.95 ☐ 0.59

3) 3.250 ☐ 2.85

4) 1.052 ☐ 1.085

5) 6.025 ☐ 6.025

6) 7.825 ☐ 7.805

7) 9.732 ☐ 9.754

8) 5.075 ☐ 5.057

9) 4.301 ☐ 4.299

10) 0.075 ☐ 0.750

11) 9.125 ☐ 9.0125

12) 0.823 ☐ 1.0082

Rounding Decimals

Step-by-step guide:

✓ We can round decimals to a certain accuracy or number of decimal places. This is used to make calculation easier to do and results easier to understand, when exact values are not too important.

✓ First, you'll need to remember your place values: For example:

$$25.6872$$

2: tens	5: ones	6: tenths
8: hundredths	7: thousandths	2: tens thousandths

✓ To round a decimal, find the place value you'll round to.

✓ Find the digit to the right of the place value you're rounding to. If it is 5 or bigger, add 1 to the place value you're rounding to and remove all digits on its right side. If the digit to the right of the place value is less than 5, keep the place value and remove all digits on the right.

Examples:

1) Round 6.7326 to the thousandth place value.

First look at the next place value to the right, (tens thousandths). It's 6 and it is greater than 5. Thus add 1 to the digit in the thousandth place.

Thousandth place is 2. $\rightarrow 2 + 1 = 3$, then, the answer is 6.733

2) 5.1024 rounded to the nearest hundredth.

First look at the next place value to the right of thousandths. It's 2 and it is less than 5, thus remove all the digits to the right. Then, the answer is 5.10.

✍ *Round each decimal to the nearest whole number.*

1) 76.455	3) 9.732	5) 6.125
2) 28.012	4) 17.65	6) 8.56

✍ *Round each decimal to the nearest tenth.*

7) 62.172	9) 6.712	11) 11.345
8) 8.076	10) 33.712	12) 2.165

Adding and Subtracting Decimals

Step-by-step guide:

- ✓ Line up the numbers.

- ✓ Add zeros to have same number of digits for both numbers if necessary.

- ✓ Add or subtract using column addition or subtraction.

Examples:

1) Add. $3.4 + 5.15 =$

First line up the numbers: $\begin{array}{r} 3.4 \\ +\,5.15 \\ \hline \end{array}$ → Add zeros to have same number of digits for both

numbers. $\begin{array}{r} 3.40 \\ +\,5.15 \\ \hline \end{array}$, Start with the hundredths place. $0 + 5 = 5$, $\begin{array}{r} 3.40 \\ +\,5.15 \\ \hline 5 \end{array}$, Continue with tenths

place. $4 + 1 = 5$, $\begin{array}{r} 3.40 \\ +\,5.15 \\ \hline .55 \end{array}$. Add the ones place. $3 + 5 = 8$, $\begin{array}{r} 3.40 \\ +\,5.15 \\ \hline 8.55 \end{array}$

2) Subtract decimals. $7.78 - 6.55 =$ $\begin{array}{r} 7.78 \\ -\,6.55 \\ \hline \end{array}$

Start with the hundredths place. $8 - 5 = 3$, $\begin{array}{r} 4.67 \\ -\,2.15 \\ \hline 3 \end{array}$, continue with tenths place. $7 - 5 = 2$

$\begin{array}{r} 7.78 \\ -\,6.55 \\ \hline .23 \end{array}$, subtract the ones place. $7 - 6 = 1$, $\begin{array}{r} 7.78 \\ -\,6.55 \\ \hline 1.23 \end{array}$.

✎ *Find the sum or difference.*

1) $21.78 - 12.22 =$

2) $18.52 + 14.62 =$

3) $81.25 - 33.45 =$

4) $99.73 - 40.25 =$

5) $12.25 + 18.99 =$

6) $43.71 + 19.71 =$

7) $53.76 - 45.80 =$

8) $37.23 - 17.45 =$

Multiplying and Dividing Decimals

Step-by-step guide:

For Multiplication:

✓ Ignore the decimal point and set up and multiply the numbers as you do with whole numbers.
Count the total number of decimal places in both of the factors.
Place the decimal point in the product.
For Division:

✓ If the divisor is not a whole number, move decimal point to right to make it a whole number. Do the same for dividend.
✓ Divide similar to whole numbers.

Examples:

1) Find the product. $0.70 \times 0.40 =$

Set up and multiply the numbers as you do with whole numbers. Line up the numbers: $\frac{70}{\times 40}$, Start with

the ones place → $40 \times 0 = 0$, $\frac{70}{\times 40} \over 0$, Continue with other digits → $40 \times 7 = 280$, $\frac{70}{\times 4020} \over 2,800$, Count the

total number of decimal places in both of the factors. (4). Then Place the decimal point in the product.

Then: $\frac{0.70}{\times 0.40} \over 0.2800$ → $0.70 \times 0.40 = 0.28$

2) Find the quotient. $2.50 \div 0.5 =$
The divisor is not a whole number. Multiply it by 10 to get 5. Do the same for the dividend to get 25.
Now, divide: $25 \div 5 = 5$. The answer is 5.

✎ Find the product and quotient.

1) $0.9 \times 0.25 =$ 5) $2.25 \times 0.45 =$ 9) $8.60 \div 5 =$

2) $1.3 \times 1.5 =$ 6) $0.85 \times 0.55 =$ 10) $3.125 \div 0.25 =$

3) $3.2 \times 0.75 =$ 7) $2.40 \div 0.8 =$ 11) $10.50 \div 1.25 =$

4) $0.84 \times 0.7 =$ 8) $12.5 \div 5 =$ 12) $42.55 \div 5 =$

Answers

Comparing Decimals

1) >
2) >
3) <
4) <
5) =
6) >

7) <
8) >
9) >
10) <
11) >
12) <

Rounding Decimals

1) 76
2) 28
3) 10
4) 18

5) 6
6) 9
7) 62.2
8) 8.1

9) 6.7
10) 33.7
11) 11.3
12) 2.2

Adding and Subtracting Decimals

1) 9.56
2) 33.14
3) 47.8

4) 59.48
5) 31.24
6) 63.42

7) 7.96
8) 19.78

Multiplying and Dividing Decimals

1) 0.225
2) 1.95
3) 2.4
4) 0.588

5) 1.0125
6) 0.4675
7) 3
8) 2.5

9) 1.72
10) 12.5
11) 8.4
12) 8.51

Chapter 5: Factoring Numbers

Math Topics that you'll learn today:

- ✓ Factoring Numbers

- ✓ Greatest Common Factor

- ✓ Least Common Multiple

Factoring Numbers

Step-by-step guide:

- ✓ Factoring numbers means to break the numbers into their prime factors.
- ✓ First few prime numbers: $2, 3, 5, 7, 11, 13, 17, 19$

Examples:

1) List all positive factors of 16.

   Write the upside-down division:
   The second column is the answer.
   Then: $16 = 2 \times 2 \times 2 \times 2$ or $16 = 2^4$

16	2
8	2
4	2
2	2
1	

2) List all positive factors of 45.

   Write the upside-down division:
   The second column is the answer.
   Then: $45 = 5 \times 3 \times 3$ or $45 = 3^2 \times 5$

45	5
9	3
3	3
1	

✎ *List all positive factors of each number.*

1) 78	5) 56	9) 52
2) 18	6) 96	10) 79
3) 39	7) 88	11) 125
4) 108	8) 66	12) 85

Greatest Common Factor

Step-by-step guide:

- ✓ List the prime factors of each number.
- ✓ Multiply common prime factors.
- ✓ If there are no common prime factors, the GCF is 1.

Examples:

1) Find the GCF for 8 and 12.

The factors of 8 are: $\{1, 2, 4, 8\}$

The factors of 12 are: $\{1, 2, 3, 4, 6, 12\}$

There is 2,4 in common,

Then the greatest common factor is: 4.

2) Find the GCF for 20 and 50.

The factors of 20 are: $\{1, 2, 4, 5, 10, 20\}$

The factors of 50 are: $\{1, 2, 5, 10, 25, 50\}$

There is 2,5 and 10 in common.

Then the greatest common factor is: 10.

✎ *Find the GCF for each number pair.*

1) 12,30	5) 22,14	9) 26,104
2) 8,20	6) 18,48	10) 16,40
3) 24,6	7) 14,84	11) 17,85
4) 15,60	8) 9,60	12) 27,90

Least Common Multiple

Step-by-step guide:

- ✓ Least Common Multiple is the smallest multiple that 2 or more numbers have in common.
- ✓ How to find LCM: list out all the multiples of each number and then find the first one they have in common,

Examples:

1) Find the LCM for 5 and 6.

   Multiples of 5: $5, 10, 15, 20, 25, 30, 35, 40, 45, 50, 55, 60$

   Multiples of 6: $6, 12, 18, 24, 30, 36, 42, 48, 54, 60$

   $LCM = 30$

2) Find the LCM for 4 and 16.

   Multiples of 4: $4, 8, 12, 16, 20, 24, 28, 32$

   Multiples of 16: $16, 32, 48$

   $LCM = 16$

✎ *Find the LCM for each number pair.*

1) 4,7	5) 12,4	9) 15,20
2) 12,20	6) 16,24	10) 14,42
3) 9,10	7) 8,10	11) 7,11
4) 8,18	8) 12,20,30	12) 8,12,20

Answers

Factoring Numbers

1) 1, 2, 3, 6, 13, 26, 39, 78
2) 1, 2, 3, 6, 9, 18
3) 1, 3, 13, 39
4) 1, 2, 3, 4, 6, 9, 12, 18, 27, 36, 54, 108
5) 1, 2, 4, 7, 8, 14, 28, 56
6) 1, 2, 3, 4, 6, 8, 12, 16, 24, 32, 48, 96

7) 1, 2, 4, 8, 11, 22, 44, 88
8) 1, 2, 3, 6, 11, 22, 33, 66
9) 1, 2, 4, 13, 26, 52
10) 1, 79
11) 1, 5, 25, 125
12) 1, 5, 17, 85

Greatest Common Factor

1) 6
2) 4
3) 6
4) 15
5) 2
6) 6

7) 14
8) 3
9) 26
10) 8
11) 17
12) 9

Least Common Multiple

1) 28
2) 60
3) 90
4) 72
5) 12
6) 48

7) 40
8) 60
9) 60
10) 42
11) 77
12) 120

Chapter 6: Integers

Math Topics that you'll learn today:

- ✓ Adding and Subtracting Integers

- ✓ Multiplying and Dividing Integers

- ✓ Ordering Integers and Numbers

Adding and Subtracting Integers

Step-by-step guide:

- ✓ Integers includes: zero, counting numbers, and the negative of the counting numbers. $\{..., -3, -2, -1, 0, 1, 2, 3, ...\}$
- ✓ Add a positive integer by moving to the right on the number line.
- ✓ Add a negative integer by moving to the left on the number line.
- ✓ Subtract an integer by adding its opposite.

Examples:

1) Solve. $(-10) - (-7) =$

Keep the first number, and convert the sign of the second number to it's opposite. (change subtraction into addition. Then: $(-10) + 7 = -3$

2) Solve. $18 + (5 - 7) =$

First subtract the numbers in brackets, $5 - 7 = -2$

Then: $18 + (-2) = \rightarrow$ change addition into subtraction: $18 - 2 = 16$

✎ *Find each sum or difference.*

1) $21 - (-17) =$

2) $(5 - 12) + (-9) =$

3) $6 + (10 - 15) =$

4) $14 + (-8) =$

5) $(60 - 25) + (-5) + 3 =$

6) $22 + (-13) + 7 =$

7) $(-15) - (3 - 12) =$

8) $17 - (-29) =$

9) $(-25) - 25 =$

10) $24 - (36 - 16) =$

11) $28 - (20 - 28) =$

12) $14 - (-7) - (-15) =$

Multiplying and Dividing Integers

Step-by-step guide:

Use these rules for multiplying and dividing integers:
- ✓ (negative) × (negative) = positive
- ✓ (negative) ÷ (negative) = positive
- ✓ (negative) × (positive) = negative
- ✓ (negative) ÷ (positive) = negative
- ✓ (positive) × (positive) = positive

Examples:

1) Solve. $(4 - 8) \times (5) =$

First subtract the numbers in brackets, $4 - 8 = -4 \rightarrow (-4) \times (5) =$

Now use this formula: (negative) × (positive) = negative
$(-4) \times (5) = -20$

2) Solve. $(-9) + (84 \div 12) =$

First divided 84 by 12 , the numbers in brackets, $84 \div 12 = 7$

$= (-9) + (7) = -9 + 7 = -2$

✎ *Find each product or quotient.*

1) $(-10) \times (-11) =$

2) $(-6) \times 8 =$

3) $9 \times (-2) =$

4) $(-12) \times (-3) =$

5) $-(8) \times (-3) \times 2 =$

6) $(7 - 2) \times (-6) =$

7) $18 \div (-3) =$

8) $(-85) \div (-17) =$

9) $(-42) \div (-6) =$

10) $81 \div (-27) =$

11) $(-84) \div 14 =$

12) $(-108) \div (-9) =$

Ordering Integers and Numbers

Step-by-step guide:

- ✓ When using a number line, numbers increase as you move to the right.
- ✓ When comparing two numbers, think about their position on number line. If one number is on the right side of another number, it is a bigger number. For example, -4 is bigger than -7 because it is on the right side of -7 on number line.

Examples:

1) Order this set of integers from least to greatest. $-6, 2, -3, -2, -8, 5$
   The smallest number is -8 and the largest number is 5.

   Now compare the integers and order them from greatest to least:
   $-8 < -6 < -3 < -2 < 2 < 5$

2) Order each set of integers from greatest to least. $15, -20, -8, 1, -4, 6$
   The largest number is 15 and the smallest number is -20.

   Now compare the integers and order them from least to greatest:
   $15 > 6 > 1 > -4 > -8 > -20$

✎ *Order each set of integers from least to greatest.*

1) $12, -2, -8, -3, 1$ ___, ___, ___, ___, ___, ___

2) $-5, -13, -3, 14, 0$ ___, ___, ___, ___, ___, ___

3) $5, -8, -11, 4, -13$ ___, ___, ___, ___, ___, ___

4) $-32, -10, 2, -4, 3$ ___, ___, ___, ___, ___, ___

✎ *Order each set of integers from greatest to least.*

5) $-2, 12, 8, -4, -9$ ___, ___, ___, ___, ___, ___

6) $25, -30, -7, -3, 10$ ___, ___, ___, ___, ___, ___

7) $31, -22, -15, 20, -1$ ___, ___, ___, ___, ___, ___

8) $16, 21, -15, -16, -21$ ___, ___, ___, ___, ___, ___

Answers

Adding and Subtracting Integers

1) 38
2) −16
3) 1
4) 6
5) 33
6) 16

7) −6
8) 46
9) −50
10) 4
11) 36
12) 36

Multiplying and Dividing Integers

1) 110
2) −48
3) −18
4) 36
5) 48
6) −30

7) −6
8) 5
9) 7
10) −3
11) −6
12) 12

Ordering Integers and Numbers

1) −8, −3, −2,1,12
2) −13, −5, −3,0,14
3) −13, −11, −8,4,5
4) −32, −10, −4,2,3

5) 12,8, −2, −4, −9
6) 25,10, −3, −7, −30
7) 31,20, −1, −15, −22
8) 21,16, −15, −16, −21

Chapter 7: Order of Operations

Math Topics that you'll learn today:

- ✓ Order of Operations

- ✓ Integers and Absolute Value

Order of Operations

Step-by-step guide:

When there is more than one math operation, use PEMDAS:

- ✓ Parentheses
- ✓ Exponents
- ✓ Multiplication and Division (from left to right)
- ✓ Addition and Subtraction (from left to right)

Examples:

1) Solve. $(6 + 9) \div (10^2 \div 20) =$

First simplify inside parentheses: $(15) \div (100 \div 20) = (15) \div (5) =$
Then: $(15) \div (5) = 3$

2) Solve. $(13 \times 3) - (17 - 12) =$

First simplify inside parentheses: $(13 \times 3) - (17 - 12) = (39) - (5) =$

Then: $(39) - (5) = 34$

✎ *Evaluate each expression.*

1) $12 + (3 \times 7) =$

2) $(-3) - (4 \times 6) =$

3) $(11 \times 5) - 30 =$

4) $(18 - 11) - (3 \times 8) =$

5) $15 + (48 \div 6) =$

6) $(26 \times 2) \div 4 =$

7) $(55 \div 5) \times (-3) =$

8) $(9 \times 4) + (36 - 25) =$

9) $71 - (12 \times 3) + 14 =$

10) $(10 \times 12) \div (48 \div 4) =$

11) $(-8) + (8 \times 7) - 35 =$

12) $(15 \times 3) \div (72 \div 8) =$

Integers and Absolute Value

Step-by-step guide:

- ✓ To find an absolute value of a number, just find its distance from 0 on number line! For example, the distance of 15 and -15 from zero on number line is 15!

Examples:

1) Solve. $\frac{|-24|}{6} \times |7 - 10| =$

First find $|-24|$, →the absolute value of -24 is 24, then: $|-24| = 24$

$\frac{24}{6} \times |7 - 10| =$

Next, solve $|7 - 10|$, → $|7 - 10| = |-3|$, the absolute value of -3 is 3. $|-3| = 3$

Then: $\frac{24}{6} \times 3 = 4 \times 3 = 12$

2) Solve. $|15 - 9| \times \frac{|-4 \times 8|}{16} =$

First solve $|15 - 9|$, → $|15 - 9| = |6|$, the absolute value of 6 is 6, $|6| = 6$

$6 \times \frac{|-4 \times 8|}{16} =$

Now solve $|-4 \times 8|$, → $|-4 \times 8| = |-32|$, the absolute value of -32 is 32, $|-32| = 32$

Then: $6 \times \frac{32}{16} = 6 \times 2 = 12$

✍ *Evaluate the value.*

1) $14 - |5 - 10| + |-6| =$

2) $|-7| - \frac{|-18|}{9} =$

3) $\frac{|-54|}{6} \times |-9| =$

4) $\frac{|-12 \times -2|}{-3} \times \frac{|-28|}{4} =$

5) $|5 \times -6| + \frac{|-25|}{-5} =$

6) $\frac{|-36|}{9} \times \frac{|-60|}{12} =$

7) $|-16 + 12| \times \frac{|-3 \times 4|}{6} =$

8) $\frac{|-8 \times 3|}{-4} \times |-5| =$

Answers

Order of Operations

1) 33
2) −27
3) 25
4) −17
5) 23
6) 13

7) −33
8) 47
9) 49
10) 10
11) 13
12) 5

Integers and Absolute Value

1) 15
2) 5
3) 81
4) −56

5) 25
6) 20
7) 8
8) −30

Chapter 8: Ratios

Math Topics that you'll learn today:

- ✓ Simplifying Ratios

- ✓ Proportional Ratios

Simplifying Ratios

Step-by-step guide:

- ✓ Ratios are used to make comparisons between two numbers.
- ✓ Ratios can be written as a fraction, using the word "to", or with a colon.
- ✓ You can calculate equivalent ratios by multiplying or dividing both sides of the ratio by the same number.

Examples:

1) Simplify. $24 : 8 =$

Both numbers 24 and 8 are divisible by 8 , $\Rightarrow 24 \div 8 = 3, 8 \div 8 = 1$,

Then: $24 : 8 = 3 : 1$

2) Simplify. $\frac{16}{64} =$

Both numbers 16 and 64 are divisible by 16, $\Rightarrow 16 \div 16 = 1, 64 \div 16 = 4$,

Then: $\frac{16}{64} = \frac{1}{4}$

✎ *Reduce each ratio.*

1) $12 : 4 =$ ___ : ___

2) $6 : 42 =$ ___ : ___

3) $54 : 9 =$ ___ : ___

4) $120 : 24 =$ ___ : ___

5) $45 : 120 =$ ___ : ___

6) $18 : 30 =$ ___ : ___

7) $25 : 60 =$ ___ : ___

8) $21 : 84 =$ ___ : ___

9) $66 : 33 =$ ___ : ___

10) $130 : 26 =$ ___ : ___

11) $32 : 54 =$ ___ : ___

12) $28 : 7 =$ ___ : ___

Proportional Ratios

Step-by-step guide:

- ✓ A proportion means that two ratios are equal. It can be written in two ways:
  $$\frac{a}{b} = \frac{c}{d}, \, a : b = c : d$$

- ✓ The proportion $\frac{a}{b} = \frac{c}{d}$ can be written as: $a \times d = c \times b$

Examples:

1) Solve this proportion for x. $\frac{8}{12} = \frac{4}{x}$

   Use cross multiplication: $\frac{8}{12} = \frac{4}{x} \Rightarrow 8 \times x = 4 \times 12 \Rightarrow 8x = 48$

   Divide to find x: $x = \frac{48}{8} \Rightarrow x = 8$

2) If a box contains red and blue balls in ratio of $5 : 12$ red to blue, how many red balls are there if 60 blue balls are in the box?

   Write a proportion and solve. $\frac{5}{12} = \frac{x}{60}$
   Use cross multiplication: $5 \times 60 = 12 \times x \Rightarrow 300 = 12x$
   Divide to find x: $x = \frac{300}{12} \Rightarrow x = 25$

✍️ *Solve each proportion.*

1) $\frac{3}{8} = \frac{12}{x}, x = $ _____

2) $\frac{4}{5} = \frac{16}{x}, x = $ _____

3) $\frac{8}{9} = \frac{32}{x}, x = $ _____

4) $\frac{1}{3} = \frac{x}{96}, x = $ _____

5) $\frac{4}{9} = \frac{x}{72}, x = $ _____

6) $\frac{1}{5} = \frac{8}{x}, x = $ _____

7) $\frac{6}{10} = \frac{24}{x}, x = $ _____

8) $\frac{2}{7} = \frac{6}{x}, x = $ _____

9) $\frac{8}{9} = \frac{x}{54}, x = $ _____

10) $\frac{7}{11} = \frac{x}{121}, x = $ _____

11) $\frac{4}{5} = \frac{x}{25}, x = $ _____

12) $\frac{6}{7} = \frac{x}{91}, x = $ _____

Answers

Simplifying Ratios

1) $3:1$
2) $1:7$
3) $6:1$
4) $5:1$
5) $3:8$
6) $3:5$

7) $5:12$
8) $1:4$
9) $2:1$
10) $5:1$
11) $16:27$
12) $4:1$

Proportional Ratios

1) 32
2) 20
3) 36
4) 32
5) 32
6) 40

7) 40
8) 21
9) 48
10) 77
11) 20
12) 78

Chapter 9: Similarity and Proportions

Math Topics that you'll learn today:

- ✓ Create a Proportion

- ✓ Similarity and Ratios

- ✓ Simple Interest

Create a Proportion

Step-by-step guide:

- ✓ A proportion contains two equal fractions! A proportion simply means that two fractions are equal.
- ✓ To create a proportion, simply find (or create) two equal fractions.

Examples:

1) Express ratios as a Proportion.
150 miles on 6 gallons of gas, how many miles on 1 gallon of gas?

First create a fraction: $\frac{150\ miles}{6\ gallons}$, and divide: $150 \div 6 = 25$

Then: 25 miles per gallon

2) State if this pair of ratios form a proportion. $\frac{3}{7}\ and\ \frac{14}{28}$

Use cross multiplication: $\frac{3}{7} = \frac{14}{28} \rightarrow 3 \times 28 = 14 \times 7 \rightarrow 84 = 98$, which is not correct. Therefore, this pair of ratios doesn't form a proportion.

✎ *State if each pair of ratios form a proportion.*

1) $\frac{5}{6}\ and\ \frac{40}{48}$

2) $\frac{2}{7}\ and\ \frac{18}{63}$

3) $\frac{8}{15}\ and\ \frac{24}{60}$

4) $\frac{4}{5}\ and\ \frac{24}{30}$

5) $\frac{2}{7}\ and\ \frac{16}{56}$

6) $\frac{5}{9}\ and\ \frac{30}{81}$

7) $\frac{1}{3}\ and\ \frac{42}{126}$

8) $\frac{2}{5}\ and\ \frac{6}{16}$

9) $\frac{12}{15}\ and\ \frac{60}{75}$

10) $\frac{11}{17}\ and\ \frac{33}{51}$

11) $\frac{5}{8}\ and\ \frac{45}{78}$

12) $\frac{7}{15}\ and\ \frac{42}{80}$

Similarity and Ratios

Step-by-step guide:

✓ Two or more figures are similar if the corresponding angles are equal, and the corresponding sides are in proportion.

Examples:

1) A girl 150 cm tall, stands 400 cm from a lamp post at night. Her shadow from the light is 100 cm long. How high is the lamp post?

Write the proportion and solve for missing side.

$$\frac{\text{Smaller triangle height}}{\text{Smaller triangle base}} = \frac{\text{Bigger triangle height}}{\text{Bigger triangle base}}$$

$$\Rightarrow \frac{100}{150} = \frac{100+400}{x} \Rightarrow 100x = 150 \times 500 \Rightarrow x = 750 \; cm$$

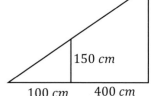

150 cm

100 cm 400 cm

2) A tree 40 $feet$ tall casts a shadow 16 $feet$ long. Jack is 5 $feet$ tall. How long is Jack's shadow?

Write a proportion and solve for the missing number.

$$\frac{40}{16} = \frac{5}{x} \to 40x = 5 \times 16 = 80$$

$$40x = 80 \to x = \frac{80}{40} = 2$$

✍ *Solve.*

1) Two rectangles are similar. The first is 8 $feet$ wide and 24 $feet$ long. The second is 12 $feet$ wide. What is the length of the second rectangle? _____

2) Two rectangles are similar. One is 5.4 $meters$ by 12 $meters$. The longer side of the second rectangle is 36 $meters$. What is the other side of the second rectangle? _____

3) A building casts a shadow 30 ft long. At the same time a girl 4.8 ft tall casts a shadow 1.6 ft long. How tall is the building? _____

4) The scale of a map of Texas is 3 $inches$: 80 $miles$. If you measure the distance from Dallas to Martin County as 15 $inches$, approximately how far is Martin County from Dallas? _____

Simple Interest

Step-by-step guide:

- ✓ Simple Interest: The charge for borrowing money or the return for lending it. To solve a simple interest problem, use this formula:

  Interest = principal × rate × time ⇒ $I = p \times r \times t$

Examples:

1) Find simple interest for $230 investment at 5% for 6 years.

   Use Interest formula: $I = prt$

   $P = \$230, r = 5\% = \frac{5}{100} = 0.05$ and $t = 6$

   Then: $I = 230 \times 0.05 \times 6 = \$69$

2) Find simple interest for $4,500 at 6% for 2 years.

   Use Interest formula: $I = prt$

   $P = \$4,800, r = 6\% = \frac{6}{100} = 0.06$ and $t = 2$

   Then: $I = 4,800 \times 0.06 \times 2 = \$576$

✎ *Determine the simple interest for these loans.*

1) $2,800 at 4% for 5 years. $ _____

2) $7,200 at 5.5% for 3 months. $ _____

3) $420 at 6% for 7 months. $ _____

4) $35,000 at 4.5% for 8years. $ _____

5) $33,000 at 4% for 4 years. $ _____

6) $14,000 at 3.5% for 5 years. $ _____

7) $15,500 at 5% for 5 months. $ _____

8) $108,500 at 2.5% for 4 years. $ _____

Answers

Create a Proportion

1) Yes
2) Yes
3) No
4) Yes
5) Yes
6) No

7) Yes
8) No
9) Yes
10) Yes
11) No
12) No

Similarity and ratios

1) 36 feet
2) 16.2 meters
3) 90 feet
4) 400 miles

Simple Interest

1) $560.00
2) $1,188
3) $176.4
4) $12,600

5) $5.280
6) $2,450
7) $3,875
8) $10,850

Chapter 10: Percentage

Math Topics that you'll learn today:

✓ Percentage Calculations

✓ Percent Problems

Percentage Calculations

Step-by-step guide:

- ✓ Percent is a ratio of a number and 100. It always has the same denominator, 100. Percent symbol is %.
- ✓ Percent is another way to write decimals or fractions. For example:

$$75\% = 0.75 = \frac{75}{100} = \frac{3}{4}$$

- ✓ Use the following formula to find part, whole, or percent:

$$\text{part} = \frac{\text{percent}}{100} \times \text{whole}$$

Examples:

1) What is 20% of 60? Use the following formula: $\text{part} = \frac{\text{percent}}{100} \times \text{whole}$

$\text{part} = \frac{20}{100} \times 60 \rightarrow \text{part} = \frac{1}{5} \times 60 \rightarrow \text{part} = \frac{60}{5} \rightarrow \text{part} = 12$

2) What is 25% of 36? Use the percent formula: $\text{part} = \frac{\text{percent}}{100} \times \text{whole}$

$\text{part} = \frac{25}{100} \times 36 \rightarrow \text{part} = \frac{900}{100} \rightarrow \text{part} = 9$

✍ *Calculate the given percent of each value.*

1) 25% of 40 = ____

2) 18% of 50 = ____

3) 40% of 70 = ____

4) 35% of 60 = ____

5) 22% of 50 = ____

6) 80% of 85 = ____

7) 16% of 40 = ____

8) 25% of 96 = ____

9) 34% of 60 = ____

10) 70% of 210 = ____

11) 45% of 120 = ____

12) 55% of 150 = ____

Percent Problems

Step-by-step guide:

- ✓ In each percent problem, we are looking for the base, or part or the percent.
- ✓ Use the following equations to find each missing section.
  - ○ Base = Part ÷ Percent
  - ○ Part = Percent × Base
  - ○ Percent = Part ÷ Base

Examples:

1) 3 is what percent of 15?

In this problem, we are looking for the percent. Use the following equation:
$$Percent = Part \div Base \rightarrow Percent = 3 \div 15 = 0.2 = 20\%$$

2) 20 is 4% of what number?

Use the following formula: $Base = Part \div Percent \rightarrow Base = 20 \div 0.04 = 500$
20 is 4% of 500.

✍ *Solve each problem.*

1) 60 is what percent of 80? ____%

2) 12 is what percent of 150? ____%

3) 16 is what percent of 40? ____%

4) 17 is what percent of 136? ____%

5) 30 is what percent of 80? ____%

6) 30 is what percent of 250? ____%

7) 120 is 40 percent of what number? ____

8) 18 is 50 percent of what? ____

9) 75 is 25 percent of what number? ____

10) 22 *is* 40 *percent of what?* ___

11) 26 *is* 40 *percent of what?* ___

12) 14 *is* 35 *percent of what?* ___

Answers

Percentage Calculations

1) 10
2) 9
3) 28
4) 21
5) 11
6) 68

7) 6.4
8) 24
9) 20.4
10) 147
11) 54
12) 82.5

Percent Problems

1) 75%
2) 8%
3) 40%
4) 12.5%
5) 37.5%
6) 12%

7) 300
8) 36
9) 300
10) 55
11) 65
12) 40

Chapter 11: Percent of Change

Math Topics that you'll learn today:

✓ Percent of Increase and Decrease

✓ Discount, Tax and Tip

Percent of Increase and Decrease

Step-by-step guide:

To find the percentage of increase or decrease:
- ✓ New Number – Original Number
- ✓ The result ÷ Original Number × 100
- ✓ If your answer is a negative number, then this is a percentage decrease. If it is positive, then this is a percent of increase.

Examples:

1) Increased by 25%, the numbers 60 becomes:

   First find 25% of 60 → $\frac{25}{100} \times 60 = \frac{25 \times 60}{100} = 15$

   Then: $60 + 15 = 75$

2) The price of a shirt increases from \$12 to \$15. What is the percent increase?

   First: $15 - 12 = 3$

   3 is the result. Then: $3 \div 12 = \frac{3}{12} = 0.25 = 25\%$

✎ *Solve each percent of change word problem.*

1) Bob got a raise, and his hourly wage increased from \$10 to \$16. What is the percent increase? _____ %

2) The price of a pair of shoes increases from \$15 to \$18. What is the percent increase? ____ %

3) At a coffeeshop, the price of a cup of coffee increased from \$0.80 \$1.00. What is the percent increase in the cost of the coffee? _____ %

4) 8 *cm* are cut from a 20 *cm* board. What is the percent decrease in length? _____ %

5) In a class, the number of students has been increased from 25 to 34. What is the percent increase? _____ %

6) The price of gasoline rose from \$1.6 to \$1.8 in one month. By what percent did the gas price rise? _____ %

7) A shirt was originally priced at \$35. It went on sale for \$43.4. What was the percent that the shirt was discounted? _____ %

Discount, Tax and Tip

Step-by-step guide:

- ✓ Discount = Multiply the regular price by the rate of discount
- ✓ Selling price = original price – discount
- ✓ Tax: To find tax, multiply the tax rate to the taxable amount (income, property value, etc.)
- ✓ To find tip, multiply the rate to the selling price.

Examples:

1) With an 12% discount, Ella was able to save $15 on a dress. What was the original price of the dress?

$12\% \ of \ x = \ 15, \frac{12}{100} \times x = \ 15, x = \frac{100 \times 15}{12} = 125$

2) Sophia purchased a sofa for $720. The sofa is regularly priced at $960. What was the percent discount Sophia received on the sofa?

Use this formula: $percent = Part \div base = 720 \div 960 = 0.75 = 75\%$

Therefore, the discount is: $100\% - 75\% = 25\%$

✍ *Find the selling price of each item.*

1) Original price of a computer: $450

   Tax: 8%, Selling price: $_____

2) Original price of a laptop: $390

   Tax: 9%, Selling price: $_____

3) Original price of a sofa: $540

   Tax: 5%, Selling price: $_____

4) Original price of a car: $32,000

   Tax: 7.5%, Selling price: $_____

5) Original price of a Table: $220

   Tax: 10%, Selling price: $_____

6) Original price of a house: $280,000

   Tax: 4.5% Selling price: $_____

7) Original price of a tablet: $380

   Discount: 12%, Selling price: $_____

8) Original price of a chair: $175

   Discount: 20%, Selling price: $_____

9) Original price of a book: $30

   Discount: 15%, Selling price: $_____

10) Original price of a cellphone: $440

   Discount: 15%, Selling price: $_____

Answers

Percent of Increase and Decrease

1) 60%
2) 20%
3) 25%
4) 40%

5) 36%
6) 12.5%
7) 24%

Markup, Discount, and Tip

1) $486,00
2) $425.10
3) $567.00
4) $34,400
5) $242.00

6) $292,600
7) $334.40
8) $140.00
9) $25.50
10) $374.00

Chapter 12:

Exponents and Variables

Math Topics that you'll learn today:

- ✓ Multiplication Property of Exponents

- ✓ Division Property of Exponents

- ✓ Powers of Products and Quotients

Multiplication Property of Exponents

Step-by-step guide:

- ✓ Exponents are shorthand for repeated multiplication of the same number by itself. For example, instead of 4×4, we can write 4^2. For $5 \times 5 \times 5 \times 3$, we can write 5^4

- ✓ In algebra, a variable is a letter used to stand for a number. The most common letters are: $x, y, z, a, b, c, m, and\ n$.

- ✓ Exponent's rules: $x^a \times x^b = x^{a+b}$, $\dfrac{x^a}{x^b} = x^{a-b}$

$$(x^a)^b = x^{a \times b}, \qquad (xy)^a = x^a \times y^a , (\tfrac{a}{b})^c = \dfrac{a^c}{b^c}$$

Examples:

1) Multiply. $4x^2 \times (-3)x^4 =$

Use Exponent's rules: $x^a \times x^b = x^{a+b} \rightarrow x^2 \times x^4 = x^{2+4} = x^6$

Then: $4x^2 \times (-3)x^4 = -12x^6$

2) Multiply. $(x^3 y^2 z\ )^5 =$

Use Exponent's rules: $(x^a)^b = x^{a \times b}$. Then: $(x^3 y^2\ z)^5 = x^{3 \times 5} y^{2 \times 5} z^{1 \times 5} = x^{15} y^{10} z^5$

✍ *Simplify and write the answer in exponential form.*

1) $2x^3 \times 4x^2 =$

2) $x^3 \times 5x^3 =$

3) $-2x^2 \times 4x^6 =$

4) $3y^2 x^2 \times 2yx =$

5) $7x^2 \times y^4 x^3 =$

6) $-3y^4 x^5 \times 2y^2 x^3 =$

7) $6y^4 x^2 \times 3x^3 y^2 =$

8) $8x^5 y^5 \times 2x^4 y^8 =$

9) $5a^2 b^2 \times 4a^2 b^2 =$

10) $2n^3 m^4 \times 7nm^4 =$

11) $x^9 y^6 \times 2x^3 y^2 =$

12) $8x^6 y^6 \times 9x^8 y^4 =$

Division Property of Exponents

Step-by-step guide:

- ✓ For division of exponents use these formulas: $\frac{x^a}{x^b} = x^{a-b}$, $x \neq 0$

$$\frac{x^a}{x^b} = \frac{1}{x^{b-a}} , x \neq 0, \qquad \frac{1}{x^b} = x^{-b}$$

Examples:

1) Simplify. $\frac{3x^5y^3}{9x^4y^2} =$

First cancel the common factor: $3 \rightarrow \frac{3x^5y^3}{9x^4y^2} = \frac{x^5y^3}{3x^4y^2}$

Use Exponent's rules: $\frac{x^a}{x^b} = x^{a-b} \rightarrow \frac{x^5}{x^4} = x^{5-4} = x,$

2) Then: $\frac{3x^5y^3}{9x^4y^2} = \frac{xy^3}{3y^2} \rightarrow$ now cancel the common factor: $y \rightarrow \frac{xy^3}{3y^2} = \frac{xy}{3}$

3) Divide. $\frac{5x^{-5}}{15x^{-4}} =$

Use Exponent's rules: $\frac{x^a}{x^b} = \frac{1}{x^{b-a}} \rightarrow \frac{x^{-5}}{x^{-4}} = \frac{1}{x^{-4-(-5)}} = \frac{1}{x^{-4+5}} = \frac{1}{x}$

Then: $\frac{5x^{-5}}{15x^{-4}} = \frac{1}{3x}$

✍ Simplify.

1) $\frac{4^3 \times 4^5}{4^2 \times 4^6} =$

2) $\frac{12x^5}{18x^4} =$

3) $\frac{6x^4}{8x^8} =$

4) $\frac{9x^8}{15x^{12}} =$

5) $\frac{21x^4y}{14xy^3} =$

6) $\frac{36x^6y^2}{12x^4y^2} =$

7) $\frac{3x^7}{5x^5y^2} =$

8) $\frac{20x^4y^2}{5x^8} =$

9) $\frac{25x^3}{20x^3y^5} =$

10) $\frac{16x^8}{12x^2} =$

11) $\frac{40x^6y^9}{12x^5y^3} =$

12) $\frac{12x^4}{16x^4} =$

Powers of Products and Quotients

Step-by-step guide:

✓ For any nonzero numbers a and b and any integer x, $(ab)^x = a^x \times b^x$.

Example:

1) Simplify. $(5x^4y^2)^2 =$

Use Exponent's rules: $(x^a)^b = x^{a \times b}$

$(5x^4y^2)^2 = (5)^2(x^4)^2(y^2)^2 = 25x^{4 \times 2}y^{2 \times 2} = 25x^8y^4$

2) Simplify. $\left(\frac{2x}{5x^3}\right)^3 =$

First cancel the common factor: $x \rightarrow \left(\frac{2x}{5x^3}\right)^3 = \left(\frac{2}{5x^2}\right)^3$

Use Exponent's rules: $\left(\frac{a}{b}\right)^c = \frac{a^c}{b^c}$

Then: $\left(\frac{2}{5x^2}\right)^3 = \frac{2^3}{(5x^2)^3} = \frac{8}{125x^6}$

✎ ***Simplify.***

1) $(3x^3y^2)^2 =$

2) $(2x^4 \times 3x^5)^2 =$

3) $(5x^3y^7)^3 =$

4) $(2x^8y^3)^4 =$

5) $(3x^6y^2)^4 =$

6) $(2xy \times 3y^5)^3 =$

7) $\left(\frac{6x^3}{x^5}\right)^2 =$

8) $\left(\frac{2x^3y^5}{x^6y^2}\right)^2 =$

9) $\left(\frac{16}{8x^{10}}\right)^3 =$

10) $\left(\frac{2x^2}{x^3y^4}\right)^4 =$

11) $\left(\frac{x^3y^4}{x^5y^2}\right)^{-3} =$

12) $\left(\frac{2x^6y^2}{x^5}\right)^{-3} =$

Answers

Multiplication Property of Exponents

1) $8x^5$
2) $5x^6$
3) $-8x^8$
4) $6x^3y^3$
5) $7x^5y^4$
6) $-6x^8y^6$

7) $18x^5y^6$
8) $16x^9y^{13}$
9) $20a^4b^4$
10) $14n^4m^8$
11) $2x^{12}y^8$
12) $72x^{14}y^{10}$

Division Property of Exponents

1) 1
2) $\dfrac{2x}{3}$
3) $\dfrac{3}{4x^4}$
4) $\dfrac{3}{5x^4}$
5) $\dfrac{3x^3}{2y^2}$
6) $3x^2$

7) $\dfrac{3x^2}{5y^2}$
8) $\dfrac{4y^2}{x^4}$
9) $\dfrac{5}{4y^5}$
10) $\dfrac{4x^6}{3}$
11) $\dfrac{10xy^6}{3}$
12) $\dfrac{3}{4}$

Powers of Products and Quotients

1) $9x^6y^4$
2) $36x^{18}$
3) $125x^9y^{21}$
4) $16x^{32}y^{12}$
5) $81x^{24}y^8$
6) $216x^3y^{18}$
7) $\dfrac{36}{x^4}$

8) $\dfrac{4y^6}{x^6}$
9) $\dfrac{8}{x^{30}}$
10) $\dfrac{16}{x^4y^{16}}$
11) $\dfrac{x^6}{y^6}$
12) $\dfrac{1}{8x^3y^6}$

Chapter 13:
Exponents and Roots

Math Topics that you'll learn today:

✓ Zero and Negative Exponents

✓ Negative Exponents and Negative Bases

✓ Scientific Notation

✓ Square Roots

Zero and Negative Exponents

Step-by-step guide:

- ✓ A negative exponent simply means that the base is on the wrong side of the fraction line, so you need to flip the base to the other side. For instance, "x^{-2}" (pronounced as "ecks to the minus two") just means "x^2" but underneath, as in $\frac{1}{x^2}$.

Example:

1) Evaluate. $\left(\frac{3}{5}\right)^{-2} =$

Use Exponent's rules: $\frac{1}{x^b} = x^{-b} \rightarrow \left(\frac{3}{5}\right)^{-2} = \frac{1}{\left(\frac{3}{5}\right)^2} = \frac{1}{\frac{3^2}{5^2}}$

Now use fraction rule: $\frac{1}{\frac{b}{c}} = \frac{c}{b} \rightarrow \frac{1}{\frac{3^2}{5^2}} = \frac{5^2}{3^2} = \frac{25}{9}$

2) Evaluate. $\left(\frac{4}{3}\right)^{-3} =$

Use Exponent's rules: $\frac{1}{x^b} = x^{-b} \rightarrow \left(\frac{4}{3}\right)^{-3} = \frac{1}{\left(\frac{4}{3}\right)^3} = \frac{1}{\frac{4^3}{3^3}}$

Now use fraction rule: $\frac{1}{\frac{b}{c}} = \frac{c}{b} \rightarrow \frac{1}{\frac{4^3}{3^3}} = \frac{3^3}{4^3} = \frac{27}{64}$

✎ ***Evaluate the following expressions.***

1) $6^{-2} =$

2) $4^{-4} =$

3) $3^{-3} =$

4) $8^{-2} =$

5) $12^{-2} =$

6) $6^{-4} =$

7) $2^{-8} =$

8) $3^{-4} =$

9) $\left(\frac{1}{3}\right)^{-2}$

10) $\left(\frac{1}{5}\right)^{-3} =$

11) $\left(\frac{3}{5}\right)^{-3} =$

12) $\left(\frac{4}{6}\right)^{-3} =$

Negative Exponents and Negative Bases

Step-by-step guide:

- ✓ Make the power positive. A negative exponent is the reciprocal of that number with a positive exponent.
- ✓ The parenthesis is important!
- ✓ -8^{-2} is not the same as $(-8)^{-2}$

$$-(8)^{-2} = -\frac{1}{8^2} \text{ and } (-8)^{-2} = +\frac{1}{8^2}$$

Example:

1) Simplify. $\left(\frac{5a}{3b}\right)^{-3} =$

Use Exponent's rules: $\frac{1}{x^b} = x^{-b} \rightarrow \left(\frac{5a}{3b}\right)^{-3} = \frac{1}{\left(\frac{5a}{3b}\right)^3} = \frac{1}{\frac{5^3 a^3}{3^3 b^3}}$

Now use fraction rule: $\frac{1}{\frac{a}{b}} = \frac{b}{a} \rightarrow \frac{1}{\frac{5^3 a^3}{3^3 b^3}} = \frac{3^3 b^3}{5^3 a^3}$

Then: $\frac{3^3 b^3}{5^3 a^3} = \frac{27 b^3}{125 a^3}$

2) Simplify. $\left(-\frac{2xy}{5y^2 z}\right)^{-2} =$

Use Exponent's rules: $\frac{1}{x^b} = x^{-b} \rightarrow \left(-\frac{2xy}{5y^2 z}\right)^{-2} = \frac{1}{\left(-\frac{2xy}{5y^2 z}\right)^2} = \frac{1}{\frac{2^2 x^2 y^2}{5^2 y^4 z^2}}$

Now use fraction rule: $\frac{1}{\frac{b}{c}} = \frac{c}{b} \rightarrow \frac{1}{\frac{2^2 x^2 y^2}{5^2 y^4 z^2}} = \frac{5^2 y^4 z^2}{2^2 x^2 y^2} = \frac{25 y^2 z^2}{4 x^2}$

✎ *Simplify.*

1) $-3x^{-3} y^{-2} =$

2) $5x^{-2} y^{-4} =$

3) $8a^{-4} b^{-3} =$

4) $-7x^5 y^{-10} =$

5) $-\frac{15y}{3x^{-4}} =$

6) $\frac{3b^{-2}}{-6c^{-6}} =$

7) $\frac{10ab}{a^{-5} b^{-6}} =$

8) $-\frac{8n^{-6}}{12p^{-8}} =$

9) $\frac{16cb^{-7}}{-12a^{-5}} =$

10) $\left(\frac{5ac}{3a^{-3}}\right)^{-2} =$

11) $\left(-\frac{4x}{12y^2 z}\right)^{-3} =$

12) $\frac{6a^3 b^{-5}}{-2ac^{-3}} =$

13) $\left(-\frac{x^5}{x^2}\right)^{-4} =$

Scientific Notation

Step-by-step guide:

- ✓ It is used to write very big or very small numbers in decimal form.
- ✓ In scientific notation all numbers are written in the form of:

$$m \times 10^n$$

Decimal notation	Scientific notation
4	4×10^0
– 36,000	-3.6×10^4
0.9	9×10^{-1}
3,283.246	$3.283,246 \times 10^3$

Example:

1) Write **0.000027** in scientific notation.

First, move the decimal point to the right so that you have a number that is between 1 and 10. Then: $N = 2.7$

Second, determine how many places the decimal moved in step 1 by the power of 10.

Then: $10^{-5} \rightarrow$ When the decimal moved to the right, the exponent is negative.

Then: $0.000027 = 2.7 \times 10^{-5}$

2) Write **5.4×10^{-7}** in standard notation.

$10^{-5} \rightarrow$ When the decimal moved to the right, the exponent is negative.

Then: $5.4 \times 10^{-7} = 0.00000054$

✍ *Write each number in scientific notation.*

1) $0.000065 =$ 3) $125,000,000 =$

2) $0.000312 =$ 4) $812,000 =$

✍ *Write each number in standard notation.*

5) $9 \times 10^{-2} =$ 7) $3.8 \times 10^5 =$

6) $7 \times 10^{-4} =$ 8) $0.25 \times 10^4 =$

Square Roots

Step-by-step guide:

✓ A square root of x is a number r whose square is: $r^2 = x$

r is a square root of x.

Example:

1) Find the square root of $\sqrt{169}$.

First factor the number: $169 = 13^2$, Then: $\sqrt{169} = \sqrt{13^2}$

Now use radical rule: $\sqrt[n]{a^n} = a$

Then: $\sqrt{13^2} = 13$

2) Evaluate. $\sqrt{9} \times \sqrt{25} =$

First factor the numbers: $9 = 3^2$ and $25 = 5^2$

Then: $\sqrt{9} \times \sqrt{16} = \sqrt{3^2} \times \sqrt{5^2}$

Now use radical rule: $\sqrt[n]{a^n} = a$, Then: $\sqrt{3^2} \times \sqrt{5^2} = 3 \times 5 = 15$

✍ *Evaluate.*

1) $\sqrt{36} \times \sqrt{16} = $ _____

2) $\sqrt{81} \times \sqrt{4} = $ _____

3) $\sqrt{49} \times \sqrt{64} = $ _____

4) $\sqrt{121} \times \sqrt{16} = $ _____

5) $\sqrt{14} \times \sqrt{14} = $ _____

6) $\sqrt{27} \times \sqrt{3} = $ _____

7) $\sqrt{5} + \sqrt{5} = $ _____

8) $\sqrt{12} + \sqrt{12} = $ _____

9) $3\sqrt{125} - 5\sqrt{5} = $ _____

10) $5\sqrt{16} \times 2\sqrt{4} = $ _____

11) $6\sqrt{3} \times 2\sqrt{3} = $ _____

12) $5\sqrt{6} - \sqrt{24} = $ _____

Answers

Zero and Negative Exponents

1) $\dfrac{1}{36}$

2) $\dfrac{1}{256}$

3) $\dfrac{1}{27}$

4) $\dfrac{1}{64}$

5) $\dfrac{1}{144}$

6) $\dfrac{1}{1296}$

7) $\dfrac{1}{256}$

8) $\dfrac{1}{81}$

9) 9

10) 125

11) $\dfrac{125}{27}$

12) $\dfrac{216}{64}$

Negative Exponents and Negative Bases

1) $-\dfrac{3}{x^3\,y^3}$

2) $\dfrac{5}{x^2 y^4}$

3) $\dfrac{8}{a^4 b^3}$

4) $-\dfrac{7x^5}{y^{10}}$

5) $-5x^4 y$

6) $-\dfrac{c^6}{2b^2}$

7) $10a^6 b^7$

8) $-\dfrac{2p^8}{3n^6}$

9) $-\dfrac{4ca^5}{3b^7}$

10) $\dfrac{9}{25a^8 c^2}$

11) $-\dfrac{27y^6 z^3}{x^3}$

12) $-\dfrac{3a^2 c^3}{b^5}$

13) $\dfrac{1}{x^{12}}$

Scientific Notation

1) 6.5×10^{-5}

2) 3.12×10^{-4}

3) 1.25×10^8

4) 8.12×10^5

5) 0.09

6) 0.0007

7) $380,000$

8) $2,500$

Square Roots

1) 24

2) 18

3) 56

4) 44

5) 14

6) 9

7) $2\sqrt{5}$

8) $4\sqrt{3}$

9) $10\sqrt{5}$

10) 80

11) 36

12) $3\sqrt{6}$

Chapter 14:
Expressions and
Variables

Math Topics that you'll learn today:

- ✓ Simplifying Variable Expressions

- ✓ Simplifying Polynomial Expressions

- ✓ Translate Phrases into an Algebraic Statement

Simplifying Variable Expressions

Step-by-step guide:

- ✓ In algebra, a variable is a letter used to stand for a number. The most common letters are: $x, y, z, a, b, c, m,$ and n.
- ✓ algebraic expression is an expression contains integers, variables, and the math operations such as addition, subtraction, multiplication, division, etc.
- ✓ In an expression, we can combine "like" terms. (values with same variable and same power)

Examples:

1) Simplify this expression. $(12x + 3x + 15) = ?$
   Combine like terms. Then: $(12x + 3x + 15) = 15x + 15$ (remember you cannot combine variables and numbers.
2) Simplify this expression. $8 - 2x^2 + 12x + 8x^2 = ?$
   Combine "like" terms: $-2x^2 + 8x^2 = 6x^2$

   Then: $8 - 2x^2 + 12x + 8x^2 = 8 + 6x^2 + 12x$. Write in standard form (biggest powers first): $6x^2 + 12x + 8$

✍ *Simplify each expression.*

1) $(4x - 5x - 13 + 24) =$

2) $(-14x - 32 - 24x) =$

3) $12x - 8 - 5x =$

4) $-7 + 3x^2 - 8x^2 =$

5) $7 - 10x^2 + 5 =$

6) $2x^2 - 4x - 9x^2 =$

7) $12x^2 - 14x - 12x^2 =$

8) $3x^2 + 8x - 9x =$

9) $5x - (15 - 12x) =$

10) $11x + (16x - 20) =$

11) $(-42x - 36) - 25x =$

12) $12x^2 + (-6x) + x =$

Simplifying Polynomial Expressions

Step-by-step guide:

✓ In mathematics, a polynomial is an expression consisting of variables and coefficients that involves only the operations of addition, subtraction, multiplication, and non-negative integer exponents of variables.

$$P(x) = a_n x^n + a_{n-1} x^{n-1} + \ldots + a_2 x^2 + a_1 x + a_0$$

Examples:

1) Simplify this Polynomial Expressions. $8x^2 + 9x^3 + 5x^4 - 13x^3 =$
   Combine "like" terms: $9x^3 - 13x^3 = -4x^3$
   Then: $8x^2 + 9x^3 + 5x^4 - 13x^3 = 8x^2 - 4x^3 + 5x^4$
   Then write in standard form: $8x^2 - 4x^3 + 5x^4 = 5x^4 - 4x^3 + 8x^2$

2) Simplify this expression. $(4x^3 - 2x^5) - (6x^5 - x^3) =$
   First use distributive property: → multiply $(-)$ into $(4x^4 - x^2)$
   $(4x^3 - 2x^5) - (6x^5 - x^3) = 4x^3 - 2x^5 - 6x^5 + x^3$
   Then combine "like" terms: $4x^3 - 2x^5 - 6x^5 + x^3 = 5x^3 - 8x^5$
   And write in standard form: $5x^3 - 8x^5 = -8x^5 + 5x^3$

✎ *Simplify each polynomial.*

1) $(6x^4 + 8x^2) - (3x + 3x^4) = $ _____

2) $(3x^4 - 7x^5) - (9x^5 + 6x^4) = $ _____

3) $(5x^2 + 9x^7) - (7x^4 + 8x^7) = $ _____

4) $12x + 5x^3 - 3(4x^2 + 6x) = $ _____

5) $(9x^4 - x^8) + 2(4x^8 - 6x^4) = $ _____

6) $(8x^9 - 4x^5) - 4(6x^5 + 2x^9) = $ _____

7) $5(4x^3 - 2x^6) - 2(4x^6 - x^2) = $ _____

8) $(6x^5 - x^6) - (2x^6 - x^5) = $ _____

Translate Phrases into an Algebraic Statement

Step-by-step guide:

Translating key words and phrases into algebraic expressions:

✓ Addition: plus, more than, the sum of, etc.
✓ Subtraction: minus, less than, decreased, etc.
✓ Multiplication: times, product, multiplied, etc.
✓ Division: quotient, divided, ratio, etc.

Examples:

Write an algebraic expression for each phrase.

1) Nine more than a number is 12.
   More than mean plus a number $= x$
   Then: $9 + x = 12$

2) 7 times the sum of 4 and x.
   Sum of 4 and x: $4 + x$. Times means multiplication. Then: $7 \times (4 + x)$

🖎 *Write an algebraic expression for each phrase.*

1) 6 multiplied by sum of 2 and a number x. _____

2) Subtract 10 from a. _____

3) 12 less than twice a number. _____

4) Four times x decreased by y. _____

5) Add 5 times of x to 9. _____

6) The square of 13. _____

7) Two time of x raised to the fifth power. _____

8) The sum of seventeen and 3 times a number. _____

9) The difference between eighty–six and b. _____

10) The quotient of twenty and a number. _____

11) The quotient of the eighteen and square of x. _____

12) The difference between x and 12 is 9. _____

Answers

Simplifying Variable Expressions

1) $-x + 11$
2) $-38x - 32$
3) $7x - 8$
4) $-5x^2 - 7$
5) $-10x^2 + 12$
6) $-7x^2 - 4x$

7) $-14x$
8) $3x^2 - x$
9) $17x - 15$
10) $27x - 20$
11) $-67x - 36$
12) $12x^2 - 5x$

Simplifying Polynomial Expressions

1) $3x^4 + 8x^2 - 3x$
2) $-16x^5 - 3x^4$
3) $x^7 - 7x^4 + 5x^2$
4) $5x^3 - 12x^2 - 6x$

5) $7x^8 - 3x^4$
6) $-28x^5$
7) $-18x^6 + 20x^3 + 2x^2$
8) $-3x^6 + 7x^5$

Translate Phrases into an Algebraic Statement

1) $6(x + 2)$
2) $a - 10$
3) $2x - 12$
4) $4x - y$
5) $5x + 9$
6) 13^2

7) $2x^5$
8) $17 + 3x$
9) $86 - b$
10) $\frac{20}{x}$
11) $\frac{18}{x^2}$
12) $x - 12 = 9$

Chapter 15:
Evaluating Variables

Math Topics that you'll learn today:

- ✓ The Distributive Property

- ✓ Evaluating One Variable

- ✓ Evaluating Two Variables

- ✓ Combining like Terms

The Distributive Property

Step-by-step guide:

✓ Distributive Property:

$$a(b + c) = ab + ac$$

Examples:

1) Simply. $(3x - 2y)(-4) =$

   Use Distributive Property formula: $a(b + c) = ab + ac$
   $(3x - 2y)(-4) = -12x + 8y$

2) Simply$(-7)(6x - 12) =$

   Use Distributive Property formula: $a(b + c) = ab + ac$
   $(-7)(6x - 12) = -42x + 84$

✎ *Use the distributive property to simply each expression.*

1) $5(7y + 4x) =$

2) $9(2a - 3b) =$

3) $(-3)(4x - 5) =$

4) $(8a - 4)(-3b) =$

5) $(-2x)(y - 6) =$

6) $(5 + 4x)2 =$

7) $(-7)(3y + 2z) =$

8) $-(-7 - 6x) =$

9) $(-8a + 6)(-b) =$

10) $(-8x)(y + 1) =$

11) $-(9 + 12x) =$

12) $(-4)(2 - 3x) =$

Evaluating One Variable

Step-by-step guide:

- ✓ To evaluate one variable expression, find the variable and substitute a number for that variable.
- ✓ Perform the arithmetic operations.

Examples:

1) Solve this expression. $5 - 4x$, $x = -4$

First substitute -4 for x, then:

$$5 - 4x = 5 - 4(-4) = 5 + 16 = 21$$

2) Solve this expression. $-14 + 8x$, $x = 2$

First substitute 2 for x, then:

$$-14 + 8x = -14 + 8(2) = -14 + 16 = 2$$

✑ *Evaluate each expression using the value given.*

1) $10 + 2x$, $x = -3$

2) $3x + 1, x = 2$

3) $7x + 5, x = -1$

4) $4x - 8, x = -2$

5) $15 - 3x$, $x = 2$

6) $5x - 12, x = 4$

7) $5x - 20, x = 4$

8) $2x + (-8), x = -6$

9) $8x - 16, x = 3$

10) $10x + 4, x = -2$

11) $19 + 3x - 4, x = -5$

12) $14 - 4x, x = 6$

Evaluating Two Variables

Step-by-step guide:

✓ To evaluate an algebraic expression, substitute a number for each variable and perform the arithmetic operations.

Examples:

1) Solve this expression. $-2x + 4y$, $x = -1, y = 2$

First substitute -1 for x, and 2 for y , then:

$-2x + 4y = -2(-1) + 4(2) = 2 + 8 = 10$

2) Solve this expression. $3(2a - 3b), a = -2, b = -1$

First substitute -2 for a, and -1 for b , then:

$3(2a - 3b) = 6a - 9b = 6(-2) - 9(-1) = -12 + 9 = -3$

✍ *Evaluate each expression using the values given.*

1) $3x - 4y$,

$x = -3, y = 2$

2) $6x + 7y$,

$x = 4, y = -1$

3) $25x - 4y$,

$x = -1, y = 5$

4) $3 + 2x - y$,

$x = 4, y = -4$

5) $14 - 3y + 4x$,

$x = -1 , y = 2$

6) $8x - 4y + 5$,

$x = 3, y = -4$

7) $3a - 6b + 7$,

$a = 3, b = 6$

8) $2a + 3(5b + a)$,

$a = -2, b = 3$

9) $2(5x + 4) - 3y$,

$x = -3, y = 4$

10) $10x + 5 - 2(7y + 2)$,

$x = 1, y = -1$

11) $3x + 4 + 5y$,

$x = -4, y = 5$

12) $3(x + y) - 4xy$,

$x = 3, y = -3$

Combining like Terms

Step-by-step guide:

- ✓ Terms are separated by "+" and "-" signs.
- ✓ Like terms are terms with same variables and same powers.
- ✓ Be sure to use the "+" or "-" that is in front of the coefficient.

Examples:

1) Simplify this expression. $(-6)(3x - 4) =$

Use Distributive Property formula: $a(b + c) = ab + ac$
$(-6)(3x - 4) = -18x + 24$

2) Simplify this expression. $(-5)(4x + 5) - 10 =$

First use Distributive Property formula: $a(b + c) = ab + ac$
$(-5)(4x + 5) - 10 = -20x - 25 - 10$

And Combining like Terms:

$-20x - 25 - 10 = -20x - 35$

✎ *Simplify each expression.*

1) $5x + 3x - 5 =$

2) $(-2)(4x + 7) =$

3) $6x + 2x + 6 =$

4) $(-8)(x + 4) =$

5) $3x - 8x + 9 =$

6) $8x + 9 - 14x =$

7) $15 - (6x + 12) =$

8) $-18x - 14x + 3x =$

9) $25x - 13 - 6x + 7 =$

10) $30x - 18x - 12 =$

11) $8 + 9x - 5 + x =$

12) $(3x + 1)(x - 2) =$

Answers

The Distributive Property

1) $35y + 20x$
2) $18a - 27b$
3) $-12x + 15$
4) $-24ab + 12b$
5) $-2xy + 12x$
6) $10 + 8x$

7) $-21y - 14z$
8) $7 + 6x$
9) $8ab - 6b$
10) $-8xy - 8x$
11) $-9 - 12x$
12) $-8 + 12x$

Evaluating One Variable

1) 4
2) 7
3) -2
4) -16
5) 9
6) 8

7) 0
8) -20
9) 8
10) -16
11) 0
12) -10

Evaluating Two Variables

1) -17
2) 17
3) -45
4) 15
5) 4
6) 45

7) -20
8) 35
9) -34
10) 25
11) 17
12) 36

Combining like Terms

1) $8x - 5$
2) $-8x - 14$
3) $8x + 6$
4) $-8x - 32$
5) $-5x + 9$
6) $-6x + 9$

7) $-6x + 3$
8) $-29x$
9) $19x - 6$
10) $12x - 12$
11) $10x + 3$
12) $3x^2 - 5x - 2$

Chapter 16:
Equations and Inequalities

Math Topics that you'll learn today:

- ✓ One–Step Equations

- ✓ Multi–Step Equations

- ✓ Graphing Single–Variable Inequalities

One–Step Equations

Step-by-step guide:

✓ The values of two expressions on both sides of an equation are equal. $ax + b = c$

✓ You only need to perform one Math operation in order to solve the one-step equations.

✓ To solve one-step equation, find the inverse (opposite) operation is being performed.

✓ The inverse operations are:

- Addition and subtraction
- Multiplication and division

Examples:

1) Solve this equation. $x - 10 = 0$, $x = ?$
   Here, the operation is addition and its inverse operation is subtraction. To solve this equation, add 10 from both sides of the equation: $x - 10 + 10 = 0 + 10$
   Then simplify: $x - 10 + 10 = 0 + 10 \rightarrow x = 10$

2) Solve this equation. $4x = 20$, $x = ?$
   Here, the operation is multiplication (variable x is multiplied by 4) and its inverse operation is division. To solve this equation, divide both sides of equation by 4:
   $$4x = 20 \rightarrow 4x \div 4 = 20 \div 4 \rightarrow x = 5$$

✎ *Solve each equation.*

1) $12 = -3 + x$, $x =$ ____

2) $2x + 7 = 3$, $x =$ ____

3) $4x - 8 = 12$, $x =$ ____

4) $16 = 26 - x$, $x =$ ____

5) $9 + 3x = -9$, $x =$ ____

6) $5x - 10 = 25$, $x =$ ____

7) $40 = 8x - 8$, $x =$ ____

8) $6x + 5 = 23$, $x =$ ____

9) $x + 9 = -12$, $x =$ ____

10) $3x + 5 = 32$, $x =$ ____

11) $x + 7 = 9$, $x =$ ____

12) $-17 = 2x + 13$, $x =$ ____

Multi–Step Equations

Step-by-step guide:

- ✓ Combine "like" terms on one side.
- ✓ Bring variables to one side by adding or subtracting.
- ✓ Simplify using the inverse of addition or subtraction.
- ✓ Simplify further by using the inverse of multiplication or division.

Examples:

1) Solve this equation. $-(4 + x) = 8$

First use Distributive Property: $-(4 + x) = -4 - x$

Now solve by adding 4 to both sides of the equation. $-4 - x = 8 \rightarrow -4 - x + 4 = 8 + 4$

Now simplify: $-4 - x + 4 = 8 + 4 \rightarrow -x = 12 \rightarrow x = -12$

2) Solve this equation. $5x - 6 = 12 + 3x$

First bring variables to one side by subtracting $3x$ to both sides.

$5x - 6 - 3x = 12 + 3x - 3x \rightarrow 2x - 6 = 12$. Now, add 6 from both sides:

$2x - 6 + 6 = 12 + 6 \rightarrow 2x = 18$

Now, divide both sides by 2: $2x = 18 \rightarrow 2x \div 2 = \frac{18}{2} \rightarrow x = 9$

✎ *Solve each equation.*

1) $-5(4 + x) = 10$

2) $6(2 + x) = 30$

3) $42 = -7\,(x - 2)$

4) $4(5 - 2x) = 44$

5) $-8 = -2(2x - 44)$

6) $3(4 + x) = 0$

7) $4(x - 5) = -8$

8) $-12 = 3x - 15x$

9) $5x + 20 = x - 4$

10) $3(4 - 2x) = -24$

11) $8 - 3x = -12 - x$

12) $3 - x = 7 + x$

Graphing Single–Variable Inequalities

Step-by-step guide:

- ✓ Inequality is similar to equations and uses symbols for "less than" (‹) and "greater than" (›).
- ✓ To solve inequalities, we need to isolate the variable. (like in equations)
- ✓ To graph an inequality, find the value of the inequality on the number line.
- ✓ For less than or greater than draw open circle on the value of the variable.
- ✓ If there is an equal sign too, then use filled circle.
- ✓ Draw a line to the right or to the left for greater or less than.

Examples:

1) Draw a graph for $x > \frac{5}{2}$

Since, the variable is greater than $\frac{5}{2}$, then we need to find $\frac{5}{2}$ and draw an open circle above it. Then, draw a line to the right.

Graph this inequality. $x \leq 3$.

✎ **Draw a graph for each**

inequality.

1) $x > -4$

2) $x \leq 6$

3) $x \geq -7$

4) $x < 10$

5) $x \geq -6$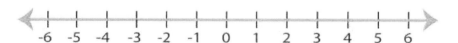

Answers

One–Step Equations

1) 15
2) −2
3) 5
4) 10
5) −6
6) 7

7) 6
8) 3
9) −21
10) 9
11) 2
12) −15

Multi–Step Equations

1) −6
2) 3
3) −4
4) −3
5) 24
6) −4

7) 3
8) 1
9) −6
10) 6
11) 10
12) −2

Graphing Single–Variable Inequalities

1)

2)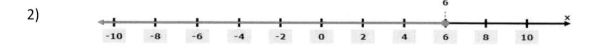

3)

4)

5)

Chapter 17:
Solving Inequalities

Math Topics that you'll learn today:

✓ One–Step Inequalities

✓ Multi–Step Inequalities

One–Step Inequalities

Step-by-step guide:

- ✓ Similar to equations, first isolate the variable by using inverse operation.
- ✓ For dividing or multiplying both sides by negative numbers, flip the direction of the inequality sign.

Examples:

1) Solve and graph the inequality. $x - 9 \geq -5$.

Add 9 from both sides. $x - 9 \geq -5 \rightarrow x - 9 + 9 \geq -5 + 9$, then: $x \geq 4$

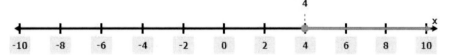

2) Solve this inequality. $x - 3 < 1$

Add 3 to both sides. $x - 3 < 1 \rightarrow x - 3 + 3 < 1 + 3$, then: $x < 4$

✎ *Solve each inequality and graph it.*

1) $4x \geq 8$

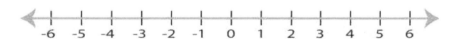

2) $2 + x \leq 3$

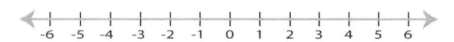

3) $3x + 5 \leq -4$

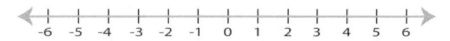

4) $5x \geq 10$

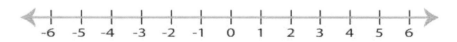

5) $7x \leq 28$

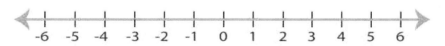

Multi–Step Inequalities

Step-by-step guide:

- ✓ Isolate the variable.
- ✓ Simplify using the inverse of addition or subtraction.
- ✓ Simplify further by using the inverse of multiplication or division.

Examples:

1) Solve this inequality. $5x + 8 \leq 3$

First subtract 8 to both sides: $5x + 8 - 8 \leq 3 - 8 \rightarrow 5x \leq -5$

Now, divide both sides by 5: $5x \leq -5 \rightarrow x \leq -1$

2) Solve this inequality. $3x - 13 \leq 5$

First add 13 to both sides: $3x - 13 + 13 \leq 5 + 13$

Then simplify: $3x - 13 + 13 \leq 5 + 13 \rightarrow 3x \leq 18$

Now divide both sides by 3: $\frac{3x}{3} \leq \frac{18}{3} \rightarrow x \leq 6$

✎ *Solve each inequality.*

1) $3x + 6 \leq 9$

2) $6x - 7 \leq 23$

3) $-9 + 7x \leq 12$

4) $5(x - 4) \leq 10$

5) $2x - 4 \leq 8$

6) $15x + 30 < -15$

7) $12x - 20 < 16$

8) $10 - 8x \geq -22$

9) $11 + 9x < -16$

10) $4 + 5x \geq 29$

11) $13 + 2x < 17$

12) $12x - 1 < 59$

Answers

One–Step Inequalities

1)
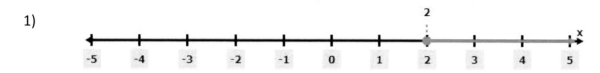

2)
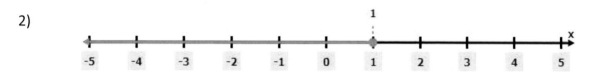

3)
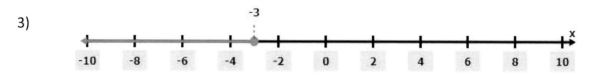

4)
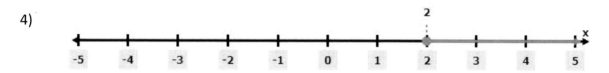

5)
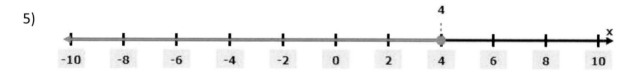

Multi–Step inequalities

1) $x \leq 1$
2) $x \leq 5$
3) $x \leq 3$
4) $x \leq 6$
5) $x \leq 6$
6) $x < -3$

7) $x < 3$
8) $x \leq 4$
9) $x < -3$
10) $x \geq 5$
11) $x < 2$
12) $x < 5$

Chapter 18:

Lines and Slope

Math Topics that you'll learn today:

✓ Finding Slope

✓ Graphing Lines Using Slope–Intercept Form

✓ Graphing Lines Using Standard Form

Finding Slope

Step-by-step guide:

- ✓ The slope of a line represents the direction of a line on the coordinate plane.
- ✓ A coordinate plane contains two perpendicular number lines. The horizontal line is x and the vertical line is y. The point at which the two axes intersect is called the origin. An ordered pair (x, y) shows the location of a point.
- ✓ A line on coordinate plane can be drawn by connecting two points.
- ✓ To find the slope of a line, we need two points.
- ✓ The slope of a line with two points A (x_1, y_1) and B (x_2, y_2) can be found by using this formula: $\frac{y_2 - y_1}{x_2 - x_1} = \frac{rise}{run}$

Examples:

1) Find the slope of the line through these two points: $(2, 4)$ and $(6, 12)$.

Slope $= \frac{y_2 - y_1}{x_2 - x_1}$. Let (x_1, y_1) be $(2,4)$ and (x_2, y_2) be $(6, 12)$. Then: slope $= \frac{y_2 - y_1}{x_2 - x_1} = \frac{12 - 4}{6 - 2} = \frac{8}{4} = 2$

2) Find the slope of the line containing two points $(-3, -3)$ and $(1, 1)$.

Slope $= \frac{y_2 - y_1}{x_2 - x_1} \rightarrow (x_1, y_1) = (-3, -3)$ and $(x_2, y_2) = (1, 1)$. Then: slope $= \frac{y_2 - y_1}{x_2 - x_1} = \frac{1 - (-3)}{1 - (-3)} = \frac{4}{4} = 1$

✍ *Find the slope of the line through each pair of points.*

1) $(5, 0), (2, 6)$

2) $(-16, 4), (0, 12)$

3) $(-4, 10), (8, -2)$

4) $(1, 3), (-2, -3)$

5) $(1, 8), (2, -8)$

6) $(-5, 3), (5, -7)$

7) $(-10, -20), (0, 0)$

8) $(-1, 5), (2, -4)$

9) $(-3, -10), (1, 6)$

10) $(-5, 4), (1, 10)$

11) $(0, -3), (5, 7)$

12) $(6, -8), (-2, 16)$

Graphing Lines Using Slope–Intercept Form

Step-by-step guide:

✓ Slope-intercept form of a line: given the slope m and the y-intercept (the intersection of the line and y-axis) b, then the equation of the line is:
$$y = mx + b$$

Example: *Sketch the graph of* $y = 4x + 1$.

To graph this line, we need to find two points. When x is zero the value of y is 1. And when y is zero the value of x is -1/4. $x = 0 \rightarrow y = 4(0) + 1 = 1, y = 0 \rightarrow 0 = 4x + 1 \rightarrow x = -\frac{1}{4}$

Now, we have two points: $(0,1)$ and $(-\frac{1}{4}, 0)$. Find the points and graph the line. Remember that the slope of the line is 8.

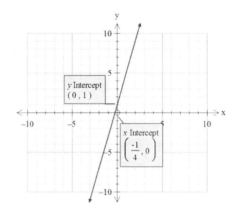

✎ *Sketch the graph of each line.*

1) $y = \frac{4}{5}x - 1$

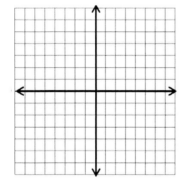

2) $y = 3 - 2x$

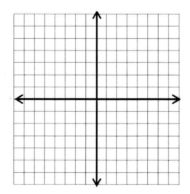

Graphing Lines Using Standard Form

Step-by-step guide:

- ✓ Find the x –intercept of the line by putting zero for y.
- ✓ Find the y –intercept of the line by putting zero for the x.
- ✓ Connect these two points.

Example:

Sketch the graph of $2x - y = -4$.

First isolate y for x: $2x - y = -4 \rightarrow y = 2x + 4$

Find the x–intercept of the line by putting zero for y.

$y = 2x + 4 \rightarrow 2x + 4 = 0 \rightarrow x = -2$

Find the y–intercept of the line by putting zero for the x.

$y = 2(0) + 4 \rightarrow y = 4$

Then: x–intercept: $(-2,0)$ and y–intercept: $(0,4)$

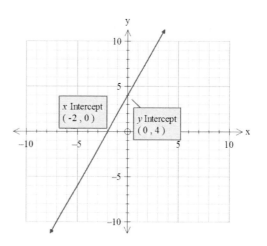

✎ **Sketch the graph of each line.**

1) $y = -\frac{2}{3}x - 5$ 2) $y = -3x + 3$ 3) $5x + 3y = 3$

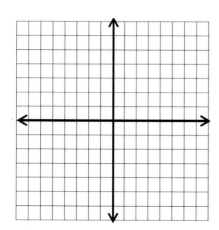 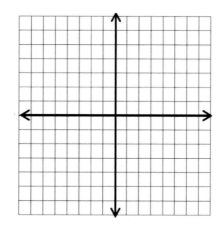 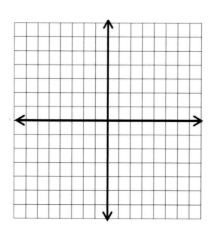

Answers

Finding Slope

1) −2
2) 0.5
3) −1
4) 2
5) −16
6) −1

7) 2
8) −3
9) 4
10) 1
11) 2
12) −3

Graphing Lines Using Slope–Intercept Form

1)

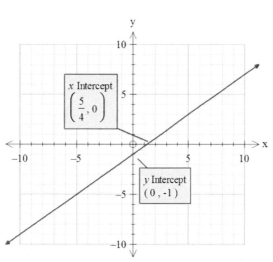

2)

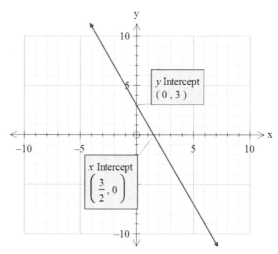

Graphing Lines Using Standard Form

1) $y = -\frac{2}{3}x - 5$

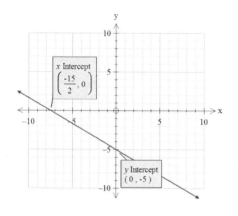

2) $y = -3x + 3$

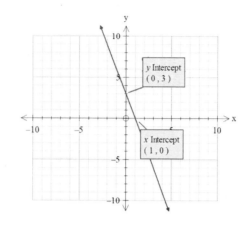

3) $5x + 3y = 3$

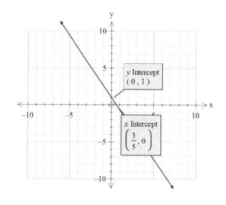

Chapter 19:
Linear Equations and Inequalities

Math Topics that you'll learn today:

- ✓ Writing Linear Equations

- ✓ Graphing Linear Inequalities

- ✓ Finding Midpoint

- ✓ Finding Distance of Two Points

Writing Linear Equations

Step-by-step guide:

- ✓ The equation of a line: $y = mx + b$
- ✓ Identify the slope.
- ✓ Find the y-intercept. This can be done by substituting the slope and the coordinates of a point (x, y) on the line.

Example:

1) What is the equation of the line that passes through $(4, -1)$ and has a slope of 3?

The general slope-intercept form of the equation of a line is $y = mx + b$, where m is the slope and b is the y-intercept.

By substitution of the given point and given slope, we have: $-1 = (3)(4) + b$

So, $b = -1 - 12 = -13$, and the required equation is $y = 3x - 13$.

2) Write the equation of the line through $(3, 2)$ and $(-5, 6)$.

$$Slop = \frac{y_2 - y_1}{x_2 - x_1} = \frac{6-2}{-5-3} = \frac{4}{-8} = -\frac{1}{2} \rightarrow m = -\frac{1}{2}$$

To find the value of b, you can use either points. The answer will be the same: $y = -\frac{1}{2}x + b$

$$(3, 2) \rightarrow 2 = -\frac{1}{2}(3) + b \rightarrow b = 2 + \frac{3}{2} = \frac{7}{2}$$

$$(-5, 6) \rightarrow 6 = -\frac{1}{2}(-5) + b \rightarrow b = 6 - \frac{5}{2} = \frac{7}{2}$$

The equation of the line is: $y = -\frac{1}{2}x + \frac{7}{2}$

✎ *Write the equation of the line through the given points.*

1) through: $(5, -3), (0, 7)$

2) through: $(-9, 8), (1, 28)$

3) through: $(5, 2), (3, 8)$

4) through: $(-1, -8), (5, 12)$

5) through: $(1, 5), (5, -13)$

6) through: $(0, 0), (5, -10)$

7) through: $(6, -4), (2, 2)$

8) through: $(7, 1), (5, 13)$

Graphing Linear Inequalities

Step-by-step guide:

- ✓ First, graph the "equals" line.
- ✓ Choose a testing point. (it can be any point on both sides of the line.)
- ✓ Put the value of (x, y) of that point in the inequality. If that works, that part of the line is the solution. If the values don't work, then the other part of the line is the solution.

Example:

Sketch the graph of $y < -x + 4$. First, graph the line:

$y = -x + 4$. The slope is -1 and y-intercept is 4. Then, choose a testing point. The easiest point to test is the origin: $(0, 0)$

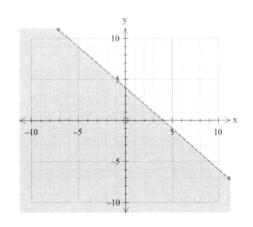

$$(0,0) \rightarrow y < -x + 4 \rightarrow 0 < -(0) + 4 \rightarrow 0 < +4$$

0 is less than 4. So, It is part of the line (on the left side) is the solution.

✏️ *Sketch the graph of each linear inequality.*

1) $y \geq 5x - 4$ 2) $y < -2x - 5$ 3) $y \leq -\frac{5}{2}x + 2$

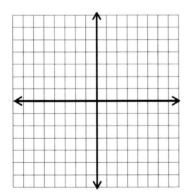 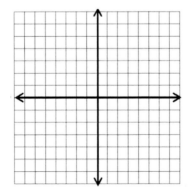 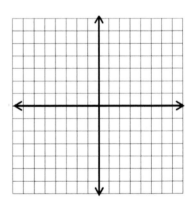

Finding Midpoint

Step-by-step guide:

- ✓ The middle of a line segment is its midpoint.
- ✓ The Midpoint of two endpoints A (x_1, y_1) and B (x_2, y_2) can be found using this formula: M $(\frac{x_1+x_2}{2}, \frac{y_1+y_2}{2})$

Example:

1) Find the midpoint of the line segment with the given endpoints. $(3, 6), (5, -4)$

Midpoint $= (\frac{x_1+x_2}{2}, \frac{y_1+y_2}{2}) \to (x_1, y_1) = (3, 6)$ and $(x_2, y_2) = (5, -4)$

Midpoint $= (\frac{3+5}{2}, \frac{6-4}{2}) \to (\frac{8}{2}, \frac{2}{2}) \to M(4, 1)$

2) Find the midpoint of the line segment with the given endpoints. $(-2, 1), (8, 3)$

Midpoint $= (\frac{x_1+x_2}{2}, \frac{y_1+y_2}{2}) \to (x_1, y_1) = (-2, 1)$ and $(x_2, y_2) = (8, 3)$

Midpoint $= (\frac{-2+8}{2}, \frac{1+3}{2}) \to (\frac{6}{2}, \frac{4}{2}) \to (3, 2)$

✎ *Find the midpoint of the line segment with the given endpoints.*

1) $(2, -3), (-6, 7)$

2) $(3, 2), (-5, 0)$

3) $(6, 1), (0, -3)$

4) $(-5, -8), (1, 4)$

5) $(-7, -2), (7, -4)$

6) $(-1, -8), (9, -6)$

7) $(9, 1), (3, 1)$

8) $(7, -8), (-3, 2)$

9) $(-7, 3), (5, 5)$

10) $(9, -10), (3, 6)$

11) $(8, -6), (2, -2)$

12) $(4, -12), (4, 16)$

Finding Distance of Two Points

Step-by-step guide:

- ✓ Distance of two points A (x_1, y_1) and B (x_2, y_2): $d = \sqrt{(x_1 - x_2)^2 + (y_1 - y_2)^2}$

Example:

1) Find the distance between of $(-3, 5), (1, 2)$.

Use distance of two points formula: $d = \sqrt{(x_1 - x_2)^2 + (y_1 - y_2)^2}$

$(x_1, y_1) = (-3, 5)$ and $(x_2, y_2) = (1, 2)$. Then: $d = \sqrt{(x_1 - x_2)^2 + (y_1 - y_2)^2} \rightarrow$

$d = \sqrt{((-3) - 1)^2 + (5 - 2)^2} = \sqrt{(-4)^2 + (3)^2} = \sqrt{16 + 9} = \sqrt{25} = 5 \rightarrow d = 5$

2) Find the distance of two points $(8, -6)$ and $(3, 6)$.

Use distance of two points formula: $d = \sqrt{(x_1 - x_2)^2 + (y_1 - y_2)^2}$

$(x_1, y_1) = (8, -6)$, and $(x_2, y_2) = (3, 6)$

Then: $d = \sqrt{(x_1 - x_2)^2 + (y_1 - y_2)^2} \rightarrow d = \sqrt{(8 - 3)^2 + ((-6) - 6)^2} =$

$\sqrt{(5)^2 + (-12)^2} = \sqrt{25 + 144} = \sqrt{169} = 13$. Then: $d = 13$

🖎 ***Find the distance between each pair of points.***

1) $(-6, 10), (2, -5)$

2) $(-7, -5), (-4, -9)$

3) $(2, -1), (-1, 3)$

4) $(-10, 0), (10, 21)$

5) $(3, -7), (9, 1)$

6) $(12, -18), (-16, 3)$

7) $(0, 5), (9, 17)$

8) $(9, 8), (4, -4)$

9) $(8, 16), (-2, -8)$

10) $(13, -6), (5, 9)$

11) $(28, -17), (13, 3)$

12) $(15, -17), (-3, 7)$

106

Answers

Writing Linear Equations

1) $y = -2x + 7$

2) $y = 2x + 26$

3) $y = -3x + 17$

4) $y = \frac{10}{3}x - \frac{14}{3}$

5) $y = -\frac{9}{2}x + \frac{19}{2}$

6) $y = -2x$

7) $y = -\frac{3}{2}x + 5$

8) $y = -6x + 43$

Graphing Linear Inequalities

1) $y > 5x - 4$

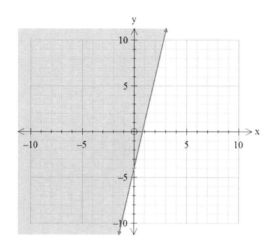

2) $y < -2x - 5$

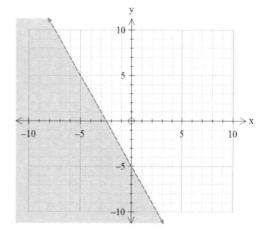

3) $y \leq -\frac{5}{2}x + 2$

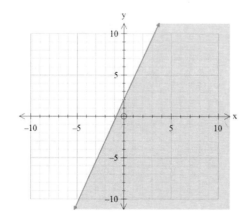

Finding Midpoint

1) $(-2, 2)$	5) $(0, -3)$	9) $(-1, 4)$
2) $(-1, 1)$	6) $(4, -7)$	10) $(6, -2)$
3) $(3, -1)$	7) $(6, 1)$	11) $(5, -4)$
4) $(-2, -2)$	8) $(2, -3)$	12) $(4, 2)$

Finding Distance of Two Points

1) 17	5) 10	9) 26
2) 5	6) 35	10) 17
3) 5	7) 15	11) 25
4) 29	8) 13	12) 30

Chapter 20:
Polynomials

Math Topics that you'll learn today:

- ✓ Writing Polynomials in Standard Form

- ✓ Simplifying Polynomials

- ✓ Adding and Subtracting Polynomials

Writing Polynomials in Standard Form

Step-by-step guide:

✓ A polynomial function $f(x)$ of degree n is of the form
$$f(x) = a_n x^n + a_{n-1} x_{n-1} + \cdots + a_1 x + a_0$$

✓ The first term is the one with the biggest power!

Example:

1) Write this polynomial in standard form. $15 + 8x^3 + 3x^5 =$

The first term is the one with the biggest power: $15 + 8x^3 + 3x^5 = 3x^5 + 8x^3 + 15$

2) Write this polynomial in standard form. $9x^4 + 3x^2 - 2x^7 - 2 =$

The first term is the one with the biggest power: $9x^4 + 3x^2 - 2x^7 - 2 = -2x^7 + 9x^4 + 3x^2 - 2$

✎ *Write each polynomial in standard form.*

1) $16x - 6x + 3 =$

2) $12 + 13x - 2x =$

3) $8x^5 + 2x^2 - 6x^4 =$

4) $14x + 5x^2 - 9 =$

5) $46x^5 + 10x^2 - 7x^3 =$

6) $12x^2 + 20x^3 - 6 =$

7) $5x - 3x^4 - 6x^7 =$

8) $-3x^3 - 4x + 7x^6 =$

9) $2x^5 + 2x + x^4 =$

10) $-2 - 4x - 3x^2 =$

11) $12x^8 - x - 2x^{10} =$

12) $13x - 3x^3 - 5x^5 =$

Simplifying Polynomials

Step-by-step guide:

✓ Find "like" terms. (they have same variables with same power).

✓ Use "FOIL". (First–Out–In–Last) for binomials:
$$(x + a)(x + b) = x^2 + (b + a)x + ab$$

✓ Add or Subtract "like" terms using order of operation.

Example:

1) Simplify this expression. $5x(3x + 6) =$

   Use Distributive Property: $5x(3x + 6) = 15x^2 + 30x$

2) Simplify this expression. $(-2x - 3)(3x + 1) =$

   First apply FOIL method: $(a + b)(c + d) = ac + ad + bc + bd$

   $(-2x - 3)(3x + 1) = -6x^2 - 2x - 9x - 3$

   Now combine like terms: $-6x^2 - 2x - 9x - 3 = -6x^2 - 11x - 3$

✎ *Simplify each expression.*

1) $7(6 - 2x) =$

2) $4x(-5x - 3) =$

3) $3x(2x + 5) =$

4) $7x(4x + 8) =$

5) $12x(2x - 6) =$

6) $(-4x)(10x + 2) =$

7) $(6x - 2)(x + 5) =$

8) $(2x - 3)(3 - 5x) =$

9) $(2x + 4)(3x + 1) =$

10) $(5x + 1)(3x - 5) =$

11) $(7x + 4)(x - 2) =$

12) $3x^2(4x + 5) =$

Adding and Subtracting Polynomials

Step-by-step guide:

- ✓ Adding polynomials is just a matter of combining like terms, with some order of operations considerations thrown in.
- ✓ Be careful with the minus signs, and don't confuse addition and multiplication!

Example:

1) Simplify the expressions. $(5x^2 - 3x^4) - (2x^4 + 6x^2) =$

First use Distributive Property for $-(2x^4 + 6x^2) \rightarrow -(2x^4 + 6x^2) = -2x^4 - 6x^2$

$(5x^2 - 3x^4) - (2x^4 + 6x^2) = 5x^2 - 3x^4 - 2x^4 - 6x^2$

Now combine like terms: $5x^2 - 6x^2 - 3x^4 - 2x^4 = -5x^4 - x^2$

2) Add expressions. $(6x^2 + 2) + (11x^2 + 3x^3) =$

Remove parentheses: $(6x^2 + 2) + (11x^2 + 3x^3) = 6x^2 + 2 + 11x^2 + 3x^3$

Now combine like terms: $6x^2 + 2 + 11x^2 + 3x^3 = 3x^3 + 17x^2 + 2$

✍ *Add or subtract expressions.*

1) $(-5x^4 - 3x) + (4x^4 + x) =$

2) $(3x^3 - 2) - (4 + 9x^3) =$

3) $(7x^5 - 4x^3) + (5x^3 - 1) =$

4) $(7x^6 - 4x^3) - (5x^6 - 5x) =$

5) $(9x^2 - 3x) + (4x^2 + 5x) =$

6) $(2x^5 - 5x) - (4x^5 - 4x) =$

7) $(8x^2 - 4x^3) - (12x^2 - 3x^3) =$

8) $(6x^6 - 9x^5) + (8x^5 - 5x^6) =$

9) $(3x^3 - 4x^2) - (4x^2 + 7x^3) =$

10) $(5x^4 - 8x) - (7x + x^4) =$

11) $(10x^7 + 5x) + (2x - 15x^7) =$

12) $(6x + 5x^2) - (4x^2 - 4x) =$

Answers

Writing Polynomials in Standard Form

1) $10x + 3$
2) $11x + 12$
3) $8x^5 - 6x^4 + 2x^2$
4) $5x^2 + 14x - 9$
5) $46x^5 - 7x^3 + 10x^2$
6) $20x^3 + 12x^2 - 6$

7) $-6x^7 - 3x^4 + 5x$
8) $7x^6 - 3x^3 - 4x$
9) $2x^5 + x^4 + 2x$
10) $-3x^2 - 4x - 2$
11) $-2x^{10} + 12x^8 - x$
12) $-5x^5 - 3x^3 + 13x$

Simplifying Polynomials

1) $-14x + 42$
2) $-20x^2 - 12x$
3) $6x^2 + 15x$
4) $28x^2 + 56x$
5) $24x^2 - 72x$
6) $-40x^2 - 8x$

7) $6x^2 + 28x - 10$
8) $-10x^2 + 21x - 9$
9) $6x^2 + 14x + 4$
10) $15x^2 - 22x - 5$
11) $7x^2 - 10x - 8$
12) $12x^3 + 15x^2$

Adding and Subtracting Polynomials

1) $-x^4 - 2x$
2) $-6x^3 - 6$
3) $7x^5 + x^3 - 1$
4) $2x^6 - 4x^3 + 5x$
5) $13x^2 + 2x$
6) $-2x^5 - x$

7) $-x^3 - 4x^2$
8) $x^6 - x^5$
9) $-4x^3 - 8x^2$
10) $4x^4 - 15x$
11) $-5x^7 + 7x$
12) $x^2 + 10x$

Chapter 21:

Monomials Operations

Math Topics that you'll learn today:

- ✓ Multiplying Monomials

- ✓ Multiplying and Dividing Monomials

- ✓ Multiplying a Polynomial and a Monomial

Multiplying Monomials

Step-by-step guide:

✓ A monomial is a polynomial with just one term, like $5x$ or $8y$.

Example:

1) Multiply expressions. $3a^2b^6 \times 6a^4b^8 =$

   Use this formula: $x^a \times x^b = x^{a+b}$

   $a^2 \times a^4 = a^{2+4} = a^6$ and $b^6 \times b^8 = b^{6+8} = b^{14}$

   Then: $3a^2b^6 \times 6a^4b^8 = 18a^6b^{14}$

2) Multiply expressions. $7x^2y^3z^5 \times (-4)x^5y^2z^7 =$

   Use this formula: $x^a \times x^b = x^{a+b}$

   $x^2 \times x^5 = x^{2+5} = x^7$, $y^3 \times y^2 = y^{3+2} = y^5$ and $z^5 \times z^7 = z^{5+7} = z^{12}$

   Then: $7x^2y^3z^5 \times (-4)x^5y^2z^7 = -28x^7y^5z^{12}$

✎ *Simplify each expression.*

1) $21xy^2 \times (-2x^2y) =$

2) $(-9y^2z) \times (2xzy^4) =$

3) $-3a^3b^5 \times 3a^3b =$

4) $3a^2b \times 5b^2c =$

5) $(-5r^3q^4) \times (4r^6q^2) =$

6) $(-4r^4s^2q) \times (3s^2q) =$

7) $5x^3y^5z \times (-x^5y^4) =$

8) $(-7 \, \alpha^3 \, \beta) \times (-\beta^6 \, \alpha) =$

9) $(-3m^3n^2) \times (7mn^6) =$

10) $3\gamma^4\delta^3 \times 5\gamma^2\delta^5 =$

11) $10u^2v^2w^4 \times (-2v^3w) =$

12) $5xyz^5 \times (-5x^2yz) =$

Multiplying and Dividing Monomials

Step-by-step guide:

- ✓ When you divide two monomials you need to divide their coefficients and then divide their variables.
- ✓ In case of exponents with the same base, you need to subtract their powers.
- ✓ Exponent's rules:

$$x^a \times x^b = x^{a+b}, \qquad \frac{x^a}{x^b} = x^{a-b}$$

$$\frac{1}{x^b} = x^{-b}, \quad (x^a)^b = x^{a \times b}$$

$$(xy)^a = x^a \times y^a$$

Example:

1) Multiply expressions. $(-7x^5)(-2x^2) =$
   Use this formula: $x^a \times x^b = x^{a+b} \rightarrow x^5 \times x^2 = x^7$
   Then: $(-7x^5)(-2x^2) = 14x^7$

2) Dividing expressions. $\frac{16x^5y^2}{4x^4y^2} =$
   Use this formula: $\frac{x^a}{x^b} = x^{a-b}, \frac{x^5}{x^4} = x^{5-4} = x$ and $\frac{y^2}{y^2} = y^{2-2} = 1$
   Then: $\frac{16x^5y^2}{4x^4y^2} = 4x$

✎ *Simplify each expression.*

1) $(8x^2y^6)(2x^2y^7) =$

2) $(-6x^2y^3)(5x^6y^3) =$

3) $(-3x^4y^3)(4x^2y^5) =$

4) $(2x^6y^3)(3x^2y^2) =$

5) $(3x^2y^8)(-3x^4y^6) =$

6) $(4x^4y^2)(-2x^3y^4) =$

7) $\frac{18x^7y^4}{6x^5y^3} =$

8) $\frac{30x^2y^8}{10x^2y^5} =$

9) $\frac{4x^8y^5}{-4x^3y^4} =$

10) $\frac{42x^6y^9}{7x^5y^4} =$

11) $\frac{72x^2y^9}{9x^2y^4} =$

12) $\frac{-24x^{16}y^{12}}{8x^{10}y^{10}} =$

Multiplying a Polynomial and a Monomial

Step-by-step guide:

- ✓ When multiplying monomials, use the product rule for exponents.
- ✓ When multiplying a monomial by a polynomial, use the distributive property.

$$a \times (b + c) = a \times b + a \times c$$

Example:

1) Multiply expressions. $-12x(2x - 3) =$

   Use Distributive Property: $-12x(2x - 3) = -24x^2 + 36x$

2) Multiply expressions. $6x(4x^5 + 2y^3) =$

   Use Distributive Property: $6x(4x^5 + 2y^3) = 24x^6 + 12xy^3$

✍ *Find each product.*

1) $(-5x^2)(2x - 3y) =$

2) $8x(-2x - 6y) =$

3) $4x(5x + 7y) =$

4) $14x(2x - 5z) =$

5) $6a(3a^2 - 3b^3) =$

6) $7y(4x - 7y) =$

7) $8y(2x + 4y - 2) =$

8) $8x^3(2x^2 - 5y^3) =$

9) $6y^2(3x - 4y) =$

10) $6y(3x^3 + 4y^5) =$

11) $7x^2(-5x^4y^3 - 12y^2) =$

12) $-4y(3x^3 - 5xy^2 + 2x) =$

Answers

Multiplying Monomials

1) $-42x^3y^3$
2) $-18xy^6z^2$
3) $-9a^6b^6$
4) $15a^2b^3c$
5) $-20r^9q^6$
6) $-12r^4s^4q^2$

7) $-5x^8y^9z$
8) $7\alpha^4\beta^7$
9) $-21m^4n^8$
10) $15\gamma^6\delta^8$
11) $-20u^2v^5w^5$
12) $-25x^3y^2z^6$

Multiplying and Dividing Monomials

1) $16x^4y^{13}$
2) $-30x^8y^6$
3) $-12x^6y^8$
4) $6x^8y^5$
5) $-9x^6y^{14}$
6) $-8x^7y^6$

7) $3x^2y$
8) $3y^3$
9) $-x^5y$
10) $6xy^5$
11) $8y^5$
12) $-3x^6y^2$

Multiplying a Polynomial and a Monomial

1) $-10x^3 + 15x^2y$
2) $-16x^2 - 48xy$
3) $20x^2 + 28xy$
4) $28x^2 - 70xz$
5) $18a^3 - 18ab^3$
6) $28xy - 49y^2$

7) $16xy + 32y^2 - 16y$
8) $16x^5 - 40x^3y^3$
9) $18xy^2 - 24y^3$
10) $18x^3y + 24y^6$
11) $-35x^6y^3 - 84x^2y^2$
12) $-12x^3y + 20xy^3 - 8xy$

Chapter 22:
Polynomials Operations

Math Topics that you'll learn today:

- ✓ Multiplying Binomials

- ✓ Factoring Trinomials

- ✓ Operations with Polynomials

Multiplying Binomials

Step-by-step guide:

✓ Use "FOIL". (First–Out–In–Last)
$$(x + a)(x + b) = x^2 + (b + a)x + ab$$

Example:

1) Multiply Binomials. $(2x - 4)(2x + 4) =$

Use "FOIL". (First–Out–In–Last): $(2x - 4)(2x + 4) = 4x^2 + 8x - 8x - 16$

Then simplify: $4x^2 + 8x - 8x - 16 = 4x^2 - 16$

2) Multiply Binomials. $(x + 8)(x - 1) =$

Use "FOIL". (First–Out–In–Last):

$(x + 8)(x - 1) = x^2 - x + 8x - 8$

Then simplify: $x^2 - x + 8x - 8 = x^2 + 7x - 8$

✎ *Find each product.*

1) $(x - 3)(x + 6) =$

2) $(x + 7)(x + 8) =$

3) $(x - 2)(x + 8) =$

4) $(x - 10)(x + 6) =$

5) $(x - 5)(x + 4) =$

6) $(x - 7)(x - 7) =$

7) $(x + 3)(x - 3) =$

8) $(x + 9)(x - 5) =$

9) $(x + 6)(x + 1) =$

10) $(x + 12)(x + 2) =$

11) $(x - 7)(x - 2) =$

12) $(x + 4)(x + 4) =$

Factoring Trinomials

Step-by-step guide:

- ✓ "FOIL":
$$(x + a)(x + b) = x^2 + (b + a)x + ab$$
- ✓ "Difference of Squares":
$$a^2 - b^2 = (a + b)(a - b)$$
$$a^2 + 2ab + b^2 = (a + b)(a + b)$$
$$a^2 - 2ab + b^2 = (a - b)(a - b)$$
- ✓ "Reverse FOIL":
$$x^2 + (b + a)x + ab = (x + a)(x + b)$$

Example:

1) Factor this trinomial. $x^2 + 2x - 15 =$
   Break the expression into groups: $(x^2 + 5x) + (-3x - 15)$
   Now factor out x from $x^2 + 5x : x(x + 5)$ and factor out -3 from $-3x - 15 : -3(x + 5)$
   Then: $= x(x + 5) - 3(x + 5)$, now factor out like term: $x + 5$
   Then: $(x + 5)(x - 3)$
2) Factor this trinomial. $x^2 - 4x - 32 =$
   Break the expression into groups: $(x^2 - 8x) + (4x - 32)$
   Now factor out x from $x^2 - 8x : x(x - 8)$, and factor out 4 from $4x - 32 : 4(x - 8)$
   Then: $= x(x - 8) + 4(x - 8)$, now factor out like term: $x - 8$
   Then: $(x - 8)(x + 4)$

✍ *Factor each trinomial.*

1) $x^2 - 2x - 24 =$

2) $x^2 + 4x - 21 =$

3) $x^2 + 3x - 54 =$

4) $x^2 - 16 =$

5) $x^2 + 4x - 60 =$

6) $x^2 - 15x + 56 =$

7) $x^2 - x - 30 =$

8) $x^2 + 7x - 18 =$

9) $x^2 - 8x - 9 =$

10) $x^2 + 19x + 88 =$

11) $x^2 - 6x - 72 =$

12) $x^2 - x - 20 =$

Operations with Polynomials

Step-by-step guide:

✓ When multiplying a monomial by a polynomial, use the distributive property.

$$a \times (b + c) = a \times b + a \times c$$

Example:

1) Multiply. $12(3x - 5) =$

Use the distributive property: $12(3x - 5) = 36x - 60$

2) Multiply. $5x(8x + 3) =$

Use the distributive property: $5x(8x + 3) = 40x^2 + 15x$

✎ *Find each product.*

1) $12(4x - 4) =$

2) $7(5x - 6) =$

3) $(-3)(11x + 3) =$

4) $-7(2x - 7) =$

5) $6x^3(8x - 1) =$

6) $7x(3x^2 - 8) =$

7) $-2x^2(-4x + 6x^2) =$

8) $6x^3 (2x + 5x^2) =$

9) $2x (x^2 - 3x + 5) =$

10) $-4(3x^2 + 9x + 2) =$

11) $-8(-2x^2 - 5x - 6) =$

12) $6x(3x^2 - x + 1) =$

Answers

Multiplying Binomials

1) $x^2 + 3x - 18$
2) $x^2 + 15x + 56$
3) $x^2 + 6x - 16$
4) $x^2 - 4x - 60$
5) $x^2 - x - 20$
6) $x^2 - 14x + 49$

7) $x^2 - 9$
8) $x^2 + 4x - 45$
9) $x^2 + 7x + 6$
10) $x^2 + 14x + 24$
11) $x^2 - 9x + 14$
12) $x^2 + 8x + 16$

Factoring Trinomials

1) $(x + 4)(x - 6)$
2) $(x + 7)(x - 3)$
3) $(x - 6)(x + 9)$
4) $(x + 4)(x - 4)$
5) $(x + 10)(x - 6)$
6) $(x - 8)(x - 7)$

7) $(x - 6)(x + 5)$
8) $(x + 9)(x - 2)$
9) $(x + 1)(x - 9)$
10) $(x + 11)(x + 8)$
11) $(x + 6)(x - 12)$
12) $(x + 4)(x - 5)$

Operations with Polynomials

1) $48x - 48$
2) $35x - 42$
3) $-33x - 9$
4) $-14x + 49$
5) $48x^4 - 6x^3$
6) $21x^3 - 56x$

7) $8x^3 - 12x^4$
8) $12x^4 + 30x^5$
9) $2x^3 - 6x^2 + 10x$
10) $-12x^2 - 36x - 8$
11) $16x^2 + 40x + 48$
12) $18x^3 - 6x^2 + 6x$

Chapter 23:
System of Equations

Math Topics that you'll learn today:

✓ Solving Systems of Equations

✓ Systems of Equations Word Problems

Systems of Equations

Step-by-step guide:

- ✓ A system of equations contains two equations and two variables. For example, consider the system of equations: $x - y = 2, x + y = 6$
- ✓ The easiest way to solve a system of equation is using the elimination method. The elimination method uses the addition property of equality. You can add the same value to each side of an equation.
- ✓ For the first equation above, you can add $x + y$ to the left side and 3 to the right side of the first equation: $x - y + (x + y) = 2 + 6$. Now, if you simplify, you get: $x - y + (x + y) = 2 + 6 \rightarrow 2x = 8 \rightarrow x = 4$. Now, substitute 4 for the x in the first equation: $4 - y = 2$. By solving this equation, $y = 2$

Example:

What is the value of $x + y$ in this system of equations? $\begin{cases} 3x - 4y = -20 \\ -x + 2y = 10 \end{cases}$

Solving Systems of Equations by Elimination: $\dfrac{3x - 4y = -20}{-x + 2y = 10}$ ⇒ Multiply the second equation by 2, then add it to the first equation.

$\dfrac{3x - 4y = -20}{2(-x + 2y = 10)} \Rightarrow \dfrac{3x - 4y = -20}{-2x + 4y = 20} \Rightarrow x = 0$. Now, substitute 0 for x in the first equation and solve for y. $3x - 4y = -20 \rightarrow 3(0) - 4y = -20 \rightarrow y = 5 \Rightarrow x + y = 0 + 5 = 5$

✎ *Solve each system of equations.*

1) $x + y = 4$ $x = $ ____

     $2x - y = 8$ $y = $ ____

2) $5x + y = 13$ $x = $ ____

     $3x - 4y = -6$ $y = $ ____

3) $3x + 2y = 5$ $x = $ ____

     $x - 4y = 11$

4) $3x - y = -8$ $x = $ ____

     $x + 3y = 14$ $y = $ ____

5) $6x + 5y = 33$ $x = $ ____

     $x - y = 0$ $y = $ ____

6) $2x + 5y = 3$ $x = $ ____

     $3x + 2y = 10$ $y = $ ____

Systems of Equations Word Problems

Step-by-step guide:

✓ Define your variables, write two equations, and use elimination method for solving systems of equations.

Example:

Tickets to a movie cost $6 for adults and $4 for students. A group of friends purchased **30** tickets for $**144.00**. How many adults ticket did they buy? ____

Let x be the number of adult tickets and y be the number of student tickets. There are 30 tickets. Then: $x + y = 30$. The cost of adults' tickets is $6 and for students it is $4, and the total cost is $144. So, $6x + 4y = 30$. Now, we have a system of equations: $\begin{cases} x + y = 30 \\ 6x + 4y = 144 \end{cases}$

Multiply the first equation by -4 and add to the second equation: $-4(x + y = 30) = -4x - 4y = -120$

$6x + 4y + (-4x - 4y) = 144 - 120 \rightarrow 2x = 24 \rightarrow x = 12 \rightarrow 12 + y = 30 \rightarrow y = 18$. There are 12 adult tickets and 18 student tickets.

✍ *Solve each word problem.*

1) Tickets to a movie cost $9 for adults and $6 for students. A group of friends purchased 24 tickets for $**174.00**. How many adults ticket did they buy? _____

2) At a store, Eva bought six shirts and eight hats for $**180.00**. Nicole bought four same shirts and two same hats for $**80.00**. What is the price of each shirt? _____

3) A farmhouse shelters 16 animals, some are pigs, and some are ducks. Altogether there are 44 legs. How many pigs are there? _____

4) A class of 300 students went on a field trip. They took 20 vehicles, some cars and some buses. If each car holds 6 students and each bus hold 24 students, how many buses did they take? _____

Answers

Systems of Equations

1) $x = 4, y = 0$
2) $x = 2, y = 3$
3) $x = 3, y = -2$
4) $x = -1, y = 5$
5) $x = 33, y = 33$
6) $x = 4, y = -1$

Systems of Equations Word Problems

1) 10
2) $14
3) 6
4) 10

Chapter 24:

Triangles and Polygons

Math Topics that you'll learn today:

- ✓ The Pythagorean Theorem

- ✓ Triangles

- ✓ Polygons

The Pythagorean Theorem

Step-by-step guide:

✓ In any right triangle: $a^2 + b^2 = c^2$

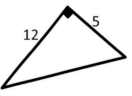

Example:

1) Find the missing length.

Use Pythagorean Theorem: $a^2 + b^2 = c^2$

Then: $a^2 + b^2 = c^2 \rightarrow 5^2 + 12^2 = c^2 \rightarrow 25 + 144 = c^2$

$c^2 = 169 \rightarrow c = 13$

2) Right triangle ABC has two legs of lengths 12 cm (AB) and 16 cm (AC). What is the length of the third side (BC)?

Use Pythagorean Theorem: $a^2 + b^2 = c^2$

Then: $a^2 + b^2 = c^2 \rightarrow 12^2 + 16^2 = c^2 \rightarrow 144 + 256 = c^2$

$c^2 = 400 \rightarrow c = 20$

 Find the missing side?

1)	2)	3)	4)
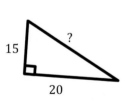	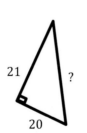	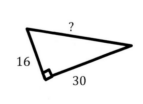	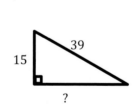
5)	6)	7)	8)

Triangles

Step-by-step guide:

- ✓ In any triangle the sum of all angles is 180 degrees.
- ✓ Area of a triangle = $\frac{1}{2}$ $(base \times height)$

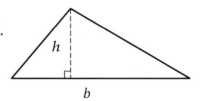

Example:

What is the area of triangles?

1)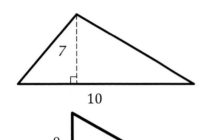

Solution:

Use the are formula: Area = $\frac{1}{2}$ $(base \times height)$

$base = 10$ and $height = 7$

Area = $\frac{1}{2}(10 \times 7) = \frac{1}{2}(70) = 35$

2)

Solution:

Use the are formula: Area = $\frac{1}{2}$ $(base \times height)$

$base = 14$ and $height = 9$

Area = $\frac{1}{2}(14 \times 9) = \frac{126}{2} = 63$

✍ *Find the measure of the unknown angle in each triangle.*

1)
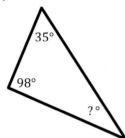

2)
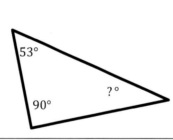

3)
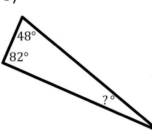

4)
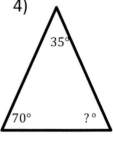

✍ *Find area of each triangle.*

5)
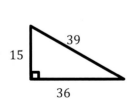

6)
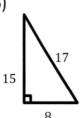

7)
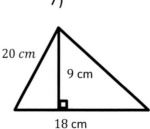

8)
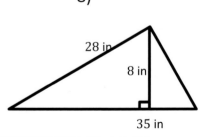

Polygons

Step-by-step guide:

Perimeter of a square $= 4 \times side = 4s$ s	Perimeter of a rectangle $= 2(width + length)$ width length
Perimeter of trapezoid $= a + b + c + d$ a d b c	Perimeter of a regular hexagon $= 6a$ a
Example: Find the perimeter of following regular hexagon. $7\,m$ $7\,m$ $7\,m$ Perimeter of Pentagon $= 6a$ Perimeter of Pentagon $= 6a = 6 \times 7 = 42\,m$	Perimeter of a parallelogram $= 2(l + w)$ l w

🖎 *Find the perimeter of each shape.*

1)

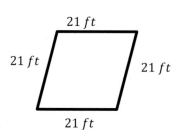

21 ft
21 ft   21 ft
21 ft

2)

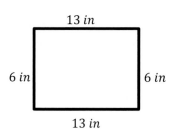

13 in
6 in   6 in
13 in

3)

14 ft   14 ft

14 ft   14 ft

4)

17 cm

5) Regular hexagon

9 m

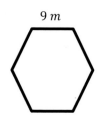

6)

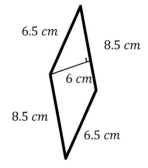

6.5 cm
8.5 cm
6 cm
8.5 cm
6.5 cm

7) Parallelogram

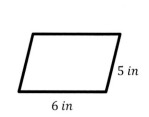

5 in
6 in

8) Square

15 m

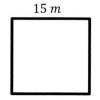

Answers

The Pythagorean Theorem

1) 25

2) 29

3) 34

4) 36

5) 10

6) 70

7) 72

8) 15

Triangles

1) 47°

2) 37°

3) 50°

4) 75°

5) 270 *square unites*

6) 60 *square unites*

7) 81 *square unites*

8) 140 *square unites*

Polygons

1) 84 *ft*

2) 38 *in*

3) 56 *ft*

4) 68 *cm*

5) 54 *m*

6) 30 *cm*

7) 22 *in*

8) 60 *m*

Chapter 25:
Circles, Trapezoids and Cubes

Math Topics that you'll learn today:

- ✓ Circles

- ✓ Trapezoids

- ✓ Cubes

Circles

Step-by-step guide:

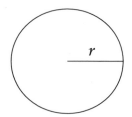

- ✓ In a circle, variable r is usually used for the radius and d for diameter and π is about 3.14.
- ✓ *Area of a circle* $= \pi r^2$
- ✓ *Circumference of a circle* $= 2\pi r$

Example:

1) Find the area of the circle.

Use area formula: $Area = \pi r^2$,

$r = 7$ then: $Area = \pi(7)^2 = 49\pi$, $\pi = 3.14$ then: $Area = 49 \times 3.14 = 153.86$

2) Find the Circumference of the circle.

Use Circumference formula: $Circumference = 2\pi r$

$r = 5$, then: $Circumference = 2\pi(5) = 10\pi$

$\pi = 3.14$ then: $Circumference = 10 \times 3.14 = 31.4$

✍ *Complete the table below.* $(\pi = 3.14)$

	Radius	Diameter	Circumference	Area
Circle 1	11 *inches*	22 *inches*		
Circle 2		18 *meters*		
Circle 3			81.68 *ft*	530.66 *square ft*
Circle 4			62.80 *miles*	
Circle 5		5 *kilometers*		
Circle 6	12 *centimeters*			
Circle 7		6 *feet*		
Circle 8				153.86 *square meters*

Trapezoids

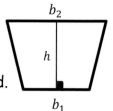

Step-by-step guide:

- ✓ A quadrilateral with at least one pair of parallel sides is a trapezoid.
- ✓ Area of a trapezoid $= \frac{1}{2}h(b_1 + b_2)$

Example:

Calculate the area of the trapezoid.

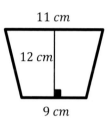

Use area formula: $A = \frac{1}{2}h(b_1 + b_2)$

$b_1 = 9$, $b_2 = 11$ and $h = 12$

Then: $A = \frac{1}{2}12(9 + 11) = 6(20) = 120 \ cm^2$

✍ *Find the area of each trapezoid.*

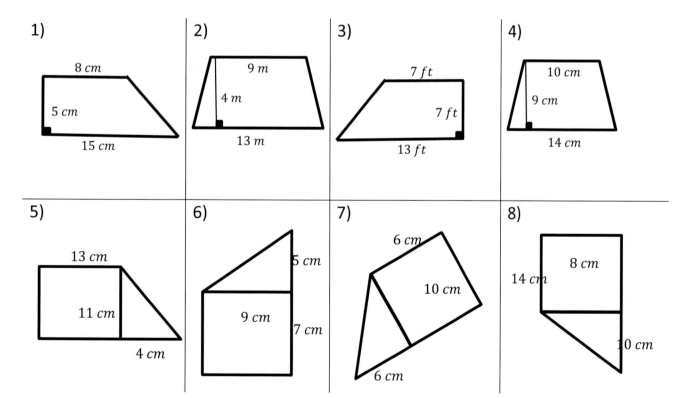

1)   8 cm   5 cm   15 cm

2)   9 m   4 m   13 m

3)   7 ft   7 ft   13 ft

4)   10 cm   9 cm   14 cm

5)   13 cm   11 cm   4 cm

6)   5 cm   9 cm   7 cm

7)   6 cm   10 cm   6 cm

8)   8 cm   14 cm   10 cm

Cubes

Step-by-step guide:

- ✓ A cube is a three-dimensional solid object bounded by six square sides.
- ✓ Volume is the measure of the amount of space inside of a solid figure, like a cube, ball, cylinder or pyramid.
- ✓ Volume of a cube = $(one\ side)^3$
- ✓ surface area of cube = $6 \times (one\ side)^2$

Example:

Find the volume and surface area of this cube.

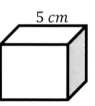

Use volume formula: $volume = (one\ side)^3$

Then: $volume = (one\ side)^3 = (5)^3 = 125\ cm^3$

Use surface area formula:

$surface\ area\ of\ cube: 6(one\ side)^2 = 6(5)^2 = 6(25) = 150\ cm^2$

✍️ *Find the volume of each cube.*

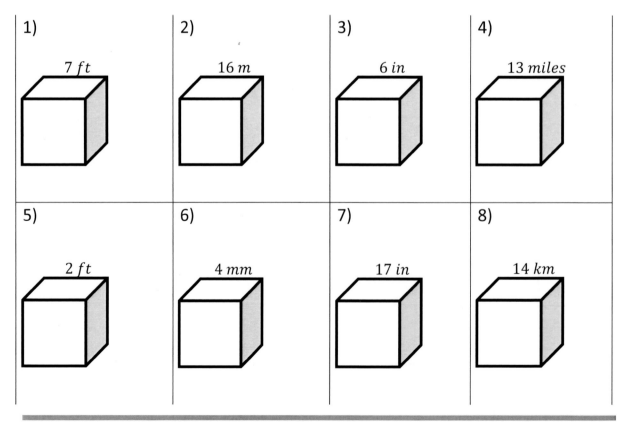

1) 7 ft

2) 16 m

3) 6 in

4) 13 miles

5) 2 ft

6) 4 mm

7) 17 in

8) 14 km

Answers

Circles

	Radius	Diameter	Circumference	Area
Circle 1	11 inches	22 inches	69.08 inches	379.94 square inches
Circle 2	9 meters	18 meters	56.52 meters	254.34 meters
Circle 3	13 square ft	26 square ft	81.68 square ft	530.66 square ft
Circle 4	10 miles	20 miles	62.80 miles	314.15 miles
Circle 5	2.5 kilometers	5 kilometers	15.7 kilometers	19.625 kilometers
Circle 6	12 centimeters	24 centimeters	75.36 centimeters	452.16 centimeters
Circle 7	3 feet	6 feet	18.84 feet	28.26 feet
Circle 8	7 square meters	14 square meters	43.96 square meters	153.86 square meters

Trapezoids

1) $57.5 \ cm^2$
2) $44 \ m^2$
3) $70 \ ft^2$
4) $108 \ cm^2$

5) 165
6) 85.5
7) 90
8) 152

Cubes

1) $343 \ ft^3$
2) $4096 \ m^3$
3) $216 \ in^3$
4) $2197 \ miles^3$

5) $8 \ ft^3$
6) $64 \ mm^3$
7) $4913 \ in^3$
8) $2744 \ km^3$

Chapter 26:
Rectangular Prisms and Cylinder

Math Topics that you'll learn today:

✓ Rectangle Prisms

✓ Cylinder

Rectangular Prisms

Step-by-step guide:

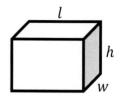

- ✓ A solid 3-dimensional object which has six rectangular faces.
- ✓ Volume of a Rectangular prism = **Length × Width × Height**

$Volume = l \times w \times h$ $Surface\ area = 2(wh + lw + lh)$

Example:

Find the volume and surface area of rectangular prism.

Use volume formula: $Volume = l \times w \times h$

Then: $Volume = 9 \times 12 \times 7 = 756\ m^3$

Use surface area formula: $Surface\ area = 2(wh + lw + lh)$

Then: $Surface\ area = 2(9 \times 12 + 12 \times 7 + 7 \times 9) = 2(108 + 84 + 63) = 510\ m^2$

✎ *Find the volume of each Rectangular Prism.*

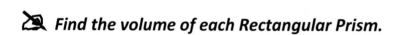

1)

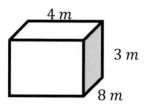

4 m
3 m
8 m

2)

14 in
9 in
8 in

3)

13 m
5 m
10 m

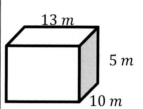

4)

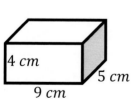

4 cm
5 cm
9 cm

5)

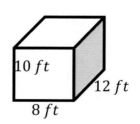

10 ft
12 ft
8 ft

6)

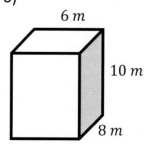

6 m
10 m
8 m

Cylinder

Step-by-step guide:

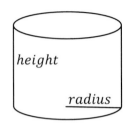

- ✓ A cylinder is a solid geometric figure with straight parallel sides and a circular or oval cross section.
- ✓ Volume of Cylinder Formula $= \pi(radius)^2 \times height \quad \pi = 3.14$
- ✓ Surface area of a cylinder $= 2\pi r^2 + 2\pi rh$

Example:

Find the volume and Surface area of the follow Cylinder.

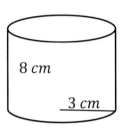

Use volume formula: $Volume = \pi(radius)^2 \times height$
Then: $Volume = \pi(3)^2 \times 8 = 9\pi \times 8 = 72\pi$
$\pi = 3.14$ then: $Volume = 72\pi = 226.08$
Use surface area formula: $Surface\ area = 2\pi r^2 + 2\pi rh$
Then: $= 2\pi(3)^2 + 2\pi(3)(8) = 2\pi(9) + 2\pi(24) = 18\pi + 48\pi = 66\pi$
$\pi = 3.14$ then: $Surface\ area = 66 \times 3.14 = 207.24$

✍ *Find the volume of each Cylinder. Round your answer to the nearest tenth.* ($\pi = 3.14$)

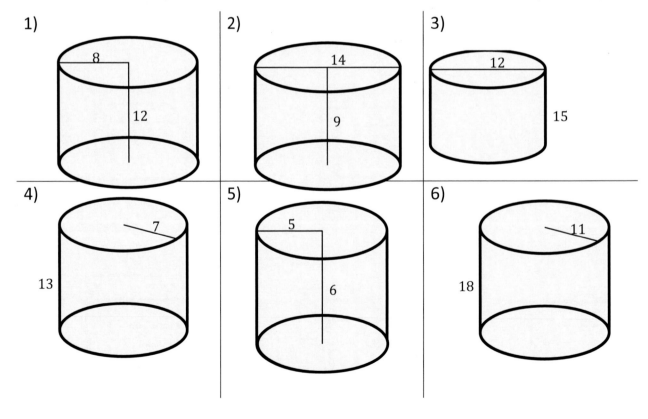

1)

8
12

2)

14
9

3)

12
15

4)

7
13

5)

5
6

6)

11
18

Answers

Rectangle Prisms

1) $96\ m^3$
2) $1008\ in^3$
3) $650\ m^3$

4) $180\ cm^3$
5) $960\ ft^3$
6) $480\ m^3$

Cylinder

1) $2411.52\ m^3$
2) $1384.74\ cm^3$
3) $1695.6\ cm^3$

4) $2000.18 m^3$
5) $471\ m^3$
6) $6838.92\ in^3$

Chapter 27: Statistics

Math Topics that you'll learn today:

✓ Mean, Median, Mode, and Range of the Given Data

✓ Bar Graph

✓ Box and Whisker Plots

✓ Stem– And– Leaf Plot

Mean, Median, Mode, and Range of the Given Data

Step-by-step guide:

- ✓ Mean: $\dfrac{\text{sum of the data}}{\text{total number of data entires}}$
- ✓ Mode: value in the list that appears most often
- ✓ Range: the difference of largest value and smallest value in the list

Example:

1) What is the median of these numbers? 8,6,4,3,5,6,11,15

   Write the numbers in order: $3, 4, 5, 6, 6, 8, 11, 15$

   Median is the number in the middle. Therefore, the median is 6.

2) What is the mode of these numbers? 13,10,5,17,14,11,5,12,10,5,15

   Mode: value in the list that appears most often
   Therefore: mode is 5

✍ *Solve.*

1) In a javelin throw competition, five athletics score 53,65,70,64 and 68 meters. What are their Mean and Median? _____

2) Eva went to shop and bought 5 apples, 8 peaches, 5 bananas, 2 pineapple and 6 melons. What are the Mean and Median of her purchase? _____

✍ *Find Mode and Rage of the Given Data.*

3) 6,7,2,10,8,6,9,11

Mode: _____   Range: _____

5) 5,6,15,21,16,18,16,20,17

Mode: _____   Range: _____

4) 12,15,17,12,19,14,16,13,12

Mode: _____   Range: _____

6) 3,5,7,14,5,12,18,23,28

Mode: _____   Range: _____

Histograms

Step-by-step guide:

✓ A histogram is an accurate representation of the distribution of numerical data.

Example:

Use the following Graph to complete the table.

Answer:

Day	Distance (km)
1	
2	

→

Day	Distance (km)
1	230
2	370
3	280
4	350
5	440

 The following table shows the number of births in the US from 2007 to 2012 (in millions).

Year	Number of births (in millions)
2007	4.1
2008	3.88
2009	4.96
2010	3.65
2011	4.15
2012	4.23

Draw a histogram for the table.

Answers

Mean, Median, Mode, and Range of the Given Data

1) Mean: 64, Median: 65

2) Mean: 5.2, Median: 5

3) Mode: 6, Range: 9

4) Mode: 12, Range: 7

5) Mode: 16, Range: 16

6) Mode: 5, Range: 25

Histograms

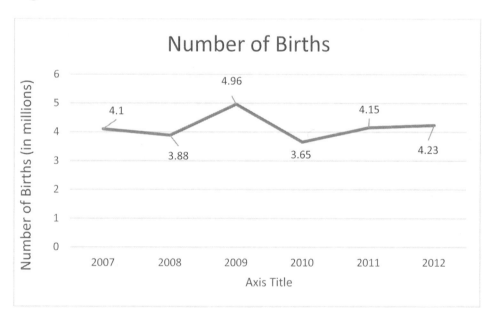

Chapter 28: Data and Probability

Math Topics that you'll learn today:

✓ Pie Graph

✓ Probability

Pie Graph

Step-by-step guide:

✓ A Pie Chart is a circle chart divided into sectors, each sector represents the relative size of each value.

Example:

A library has 1200 books that include Mathematics, Physics, Chemistry, English and History. Use following graph to answer question.

What is the number of Mathematics books?

Number of total books = 1200,
Percent of Mathematics books = 23% = 0.23
Then: $0.23 \times 1200 = 276$

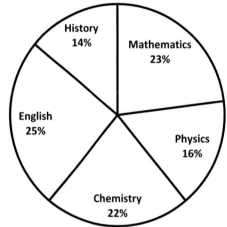

🖎 **The circle graph below shows all Jason's expenses for last month. Jason spent $800 on his bills last month.**

1) How much did Jason spend on his car last month? _____

2) How much did Jason spend for foods last month? _____

3) How much did Jason spend on his rent last month? _____

4) What fraction is Jason's expenses for his bills and Car out of his total expenses last month?

CHART JASON'S MONTHLY EXPENSES

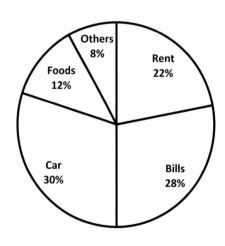

Probability Problems

Step-by-step guide:

- ✓ Probability is the likelihood of something happening in the future. It is expressed as a number between zero (can never happen) to 1 (will always happen).
- ✓ Probability can be expressed as a fraction, a decimal, or a percent.

Example:

1) If there are 7 red balls and 14 blue balls in a basket, what is the probability that John will pick out a red ball from the basket?

There are 7 red ball and 21 are total number of balls. Therefore, probability that John will pick out a red ball from the basket is 7out of 21 or $\frac{7}{7+14} = \frac{7}{21} = \frac{1}{3}$.

2) A bag contains 25 balls: two green, five black, nine blue, six brown, two red and one white. If 24 balls are removed from the bag at random, what is the probability that a brown ball has been removed?

If 24 balls are removed from the bag at random, there will be one ball in the bag.

The probability of choosing a brown ball is 1 out of 25. Therefore, the probability of not choosing a brown ball is 24 out of 25 and the probability of having not a brown ball after removing 24 balls is the same.

✍ *Solve.*

1) A number is chosen at random from 6 to 20. Find the probability of selecting number 10 or smaller numbers. _____

2) Bag A contains 7 red marbles and 5 green marbles. Bag B contains 12 black marbles and 16 orange marbles. What is the probability of selecting a green marble at random from bag A? What is the probability of selecting a black marble at random from Bag B? _____ _____

Answers

Pie Graph

1) $240
2) $96
3) $176
4) $\frac{29}{50}$

Probability Problems

1) $\frac{1}{3}$

2) $\frac{5}{12}, \frac{3}{7}$

FSA Test Review

Beginning in 2015, The FCAT test was replaced by the Florida Standards Assessments (FAS). It is the state's testing program and is based on state curriculum standards in core subjects including:

- ✓ Reading,
- ✓ Writing,
- ✓ and Mathematics.

The tests measure the progress of students from 3rd grade to 10th grade. The test window for FSA for the year 2019 is as follows:

- Grade 4 to 10 ELA Writing and Grade 3 ELA Reading: April 1–12, 2019
- Grades 4–6 ELA Reading and Grades 3–6 Mathematics: May 1–14, 2019
- Grades 7–10 ELA Reading and Grades 7 & 8 Mathematics: May 1–29, 2019

FSA Mathematics sessions are administered over two days. Test session lengths are as

follows:

Mathematics
- ✓ Grades 3–5: Two 80-minute sessions
- ✓ Grades 6–8: Three 60-minute sessions

In this book, we have reviewed all mathematics topics being covered on the FSA test for grade 8. Here, there are two complete Grade 8 FSA Math Tests. Take these tests to see what score you'll be able to receive on a real FSA Math test.

Good luck!

FSA Mathematics Practice Tests

Time to Test

Time to refine your skill with a practice examination

Take a practice FSA Math Test for grade 8 to simulate the test day experience. After you've finished, evaluate your test using the answer key.

Before You Start

- You'll need a pencil, scratch papers and a calculator to take the test.

- It's okay to guess. You won't lose any points if you're wrong.

- After you've finished the test, review the answer key to see where you went wrong.

- **Graphing Calculators are NOT permitted for the first session of the FSA Test Grade 8.**

- For each multiple-choice question, there are four possible answers. Choose which one is best. For grids in questions, write your answer in the answer boxes at the top of the grid. Then, as shown below fill in a bubble under each box in which you wrote your answer.

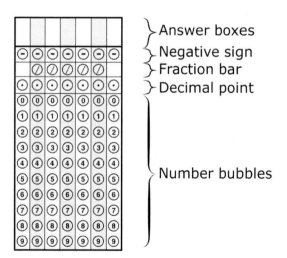

Good Luck!

FSA Math Practice

Test 1

The Florida Standards Assessments

Grade 8

Mathematics

2019

Grade 8 FSA Mathematics Reference Sheet

Customary Conversions

1 foot = 12 inches

1 yard = 3 feet

1 mile = 5,280 feet

1 mile = 1,760 yards

1 cup = 8 fluid ounces

1 pint = 2 cups

1 quart = 2 pints

1 gallon = 4 quarts

1 pound = 16 ounces

1 ton = 2,000 pounds

Metric Conversions

1 meter = 100 centimeters

1 meter = 1000 millimeters

1 kilometer = 1000 meters

1 liter = 1000 milliliters

1 gram = 1000 milligrams

1 kilogram = 1000 grams

Time Conversions

1 minute = 60 seconds

1 hour = 60 minutes

1 day = 24 hours

1 year = 365 days

1 year = 52 weeks

Formulas

Area of parallelogram =

base × height

Area of Rectangle =

Length × Width

Volume = *base × height*

Volume of pyramid = $\frac{1}{3}$ Bh

Scientific Calculators are NOT permitted for Session 1.

Time for Session 1: 60 Minutes

Session 1

1) A pizza cut into 8 slices. Jason and his sister Eva ordered two pizzas. Jason ate $\frac{1}{2}$ of his pizza and Eva ate $\frac{3}{4}$ of her pizza. What part of the two pizzas was left?

A. $\frac{1}{2}$

C. $\frac{3}{8}$

B. $\frac{1}{3}$

D. $\frac{5}{8}$

2) Robert is preparing to run a marathon. He runs $3\frac{1}{10}$ miles on Saturday and two times that many on Monday and Wednesday. Robert wants to run a total of 18 miles this week. How many more miles does he need to run? Write your answer in the box below.

3) 20 more than twice a positive integer is 68 What is the integer?

A. 24

C. 26

B. 28

D. 30

4) $[3 \times (-21) + (5 \times 2)] - (-25) + [(-3) \times 6] \div 2 = ?$

Write your answer in the box below.

5) A girl 160cm tall, stands 380cm from a lamp post at night. Her shadow from the light is 100cm long. How high is the lamp post?

Write your answer in the box below.

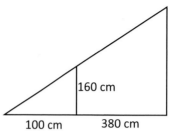

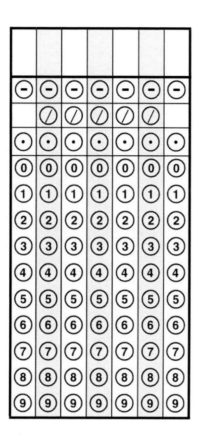

6) If a tree casts a 38ft shadow at the same time that a yardstick casts a 2ft shadow, what is the height of the tree?

A. 24ft.

B. 27ft.

C. 57ft.

D. 48ft.

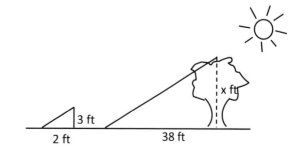

7) Mike is 7.5 miles ahead of Julia running at 5.5 miles per hour and Julia is running at the speed of 8 miles per hour. How long does it take Julia to catch Mike?

A. 2 hours

B. 5.5 hours

C. 7.5 hours

D. 3 hours

8) A company pays its employer $7,000 plus 2% of all sales profit. If x is the number of all sales profit, which of the following represents the employer's revenue?

A. $0.02x$

B. $0.98x - 7,000$

C. $0.02x + 7,000$

D. $0.98x + 7,000$

9) Jason needs an 75% average in his writing class to pass. On his first 4 exams, he earned scores of 68%, 72%, 85%, and 90%. What is the minimum score Jason can earn on his fifth and final test to pass?

Write your answer in the box below.

10) If 25% of a number is 8, what is the number?

    A. 34

    B. 32

    C. 36

    D. 30

This is the end of Session 1

Scientific Calculators are permitted for Session 2.

Time for Session 2: 60 Minutes

Session 2

11) An angle is equal to one fifth of its supplement. What is the measure of that angle?

A. 20   C. 45

B. 30   D. 60

12) Which graph shows linear equation $y = x + 1$?

A.   B.

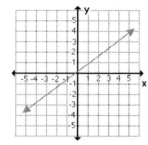 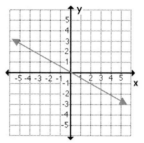

C.   D.

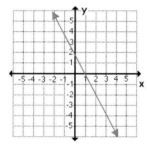 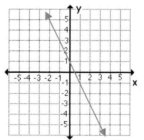

13) What is the solution of the following system of equations?

$$\begin{cases} \dfrac{-x}{2} + \dfrac{y}{4} = 1 \\ \dfrac{-5y}{6} + 2x = 4 \end{cases}$$

A. $x = 48, y = 22$ C. $x = 20, y = 50$

B. $x = 50, y = 20$ D. $x = 22, y = 48$

14) Which of the following values for x and y satisfy the following system of equations?

$$\begin{cases} x + 4y = 10 \\ 5x + 10y = 20 \end{cases}$$

A. $x = 3, y = 2$ C. $x = -2, y = 3$

B. $x = 2, y - 3$ D. $x = 3, y = -2$

15) The average of 21, 18, 16 and x is 20. What is the value of x?

A. 23   C. 30

B. 25   D. 20

16) Which of the equation represents the compound inequality?

$$5 \le 3x - 1 < 11$$

A. $3 \le x < 5$ C. $2 \le x < 6$

B. $2 \le x < 4$ D. $1 \le x < 4$

17) Point A $(-2, 6)$ and point B $(13, -2)$ are located on a coordinate grid. Which measurement is closest to the distance between point A and point B?

A.   8 units   C.   15 units

B.   13 units   D.   17 units

18) Point A $(9,7)$ and point B $(4,-5)$ are located on a coordinate grid. Which measurement is closest to the distance between point A and point B?

   A. 8 units

   B. 13 units

   C. 15 units

   D. 17 units

19) In the xy-plane, the point $(-8,8)$ and $(4,-10)$ are on line A. Which of the following equations of lines is parallel to line A?

   A. $y = \frac{3}{2}x + 4$

   B. $y = \frac{x}{2} - 3$

   C. $y = 2x + 4$

   D. $y = -\frac{3}{2}x - 4$

20) What is the x-intercept of the line with equation $10x - 4y = 5$?

   A. -5

   B. -2

   C. $\frac{1}{2}$

   D. $\frac{5}{4}$

This is the end of Session 2

Scientific Calculators are permitted for Session 3.

Time for Session 3: 60 Minutes

Session 3

21) Giselle works as a carpenter and as a blacksmith. She earns $20 as a carpenter and $25 as a blacksmith. Last week, Giselle worked both jobs for a total of 30 hours and earned a total of $690. How long did Giselle work as a carpenter last week, and how long did she work as a blacksmith?

A. $(12, 20)$ C. $(12, 18)$

B. $(10, 18)$ D. $(14, 16)$

22) Which of the following values for x and y satisfy the following system of equations?

$$\begin{cases} 3x + y = 8 \\ -5x - 2y = 0 \end{cases}$$

A. $x = 16, y = 20$ C. $x = 12, y = 40$

B. $x = -16, y = 35$ D. $x = 16, y = -40$

23) A ride in a taxicab costs $1.25 for the first mile and $1.15 for each additional mile. Which of the following could be used to calculate the total cost y of a ride that was x miles?

A. $x = 1.25(y - 1) + 1.15$ C. $y = 1.25(x - 1) + 1.15$

B. $x = 1.15(y - 1) + 1.25$ D. $y = 1.15(x - 1) + 1.25$

24) A caterer charges $120 to cater a party for 15 people and $200 for 25 people. Assume that the cost, y, is a linear function of the number of x people. Write an equation in slope-intercept form for this function. What does the slope represent? How much would a party for 40 people cost?

A. $280   C. $300

B. $330   D. $320

25) An attorney charges a fixed fee on $250 for an initial meeting and $150 per hour for all hours worked after that. Write a linear equation representation of the cost of hiring this attorney. Find the charge for 25 hours of work.

    A. $4000.00

    B. $4200.00

    C. $3800.00

    D. $4600.00

26) The sum of two numbers is 30. One of the numbers exceeds the other by 8. Find the numbers.

    A. 9,15

    B. 12,20

    C. 10,18

    D. 11,19

27) How is this number written in scientific notation?

$$0.0000005823$$

    A. 0.5823×10^{-10}

    B. 5.823×10^{-6}

    C. 5.823×10^{-7}

    D. 58.23×10^{-5}

28) How is this number written in scientific notation?

$$28,000,000,000$$

    A. 2.8×10^{9}

    B. 2.8×10^{10}

    C. 28×10^{12}

    D. 2.8×10^{8}

29) Calculate the area shaded region.

    A: $2950mm^2$

    B: $2940mm^2$

    C: $3000mm^2$

    D: $2930mm^2$

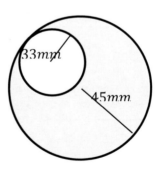

30) A circle is graphed on a coordinate grid and then reflected across the y-axis. If the center of the circle was located at (x, y), which ordered pair represents the new center after the transformation?

A. (x, y)

B. $(x, -y)$

C. $(-x, y)$

D. $(-x, -y)$

This is the end of Session 3

This is the End of Practice Test 1.   STOP

FSA Math Practice Test 2

The Florida Standards Assessments

Grade 8

Mathematics

2019

Grade 8 FSA Mathematics Reference Sheet

Customary Conversions

1 foot = 12 inches

1 yard = 3 feet

1 mile = 5,280 feet

1 mile = 1,760 yards

1 cup = 8 fluid ounces

1 pint = 2 cups

1 quart = 2 pints

1 gallon = 4 quarts

1 pound = 16 ounces

1 ton = 2,000 pounds

Metric Conversions

1 meter = 100 centimeters

1 meter = 1000 millimeters

1 kilometer = 1000 meters

1 liter = 1000 milliliters

1 gram = 1000 milligrams

1 kilogram = 1000 grams

Time Conversions

1 minute = 60 seconds

1 hour = 60 minutes

1 day = 24 hours

1 year = 365 days

1 year = 52 weeks

Formulas

Area of parallelogram =

base × height

Area of Rectangle =

Length × Width

Volume = *base × height*

Volume of pyramid = $\frac{1}{3}$ Bh

Scientific Calculators are NOT permitted for Session 1.

Time for Session 1: 60 Minutes

Session 1

1) Write the equation of a line with a slope of 5 and a y-intercept of $(0, -7)$.

A: $y = 5x - 7$ C: $y = 4x - 7$

B: $y = 5x - 4$ D: $y = 5x - 6$

2) A shirt costing $350 is discounted 15%. After a month, the shirt is discounted another 10%. Which of the following expressions can be used to find the selling price of the shirt?

A. $(350)(0.75)$ C. $(350)(0.15) - (350)(0.15)$

B. $(350) - 350(0.25)$ D. $(350)(0.85)(0.90)$

3) When a number is subtracted from 32 and the difference is divided by that number, the result is 7. What is the value of the number?

A. 6   C. 4

B. 2   D. 3

4) John traveled 240 km in 6 hours and Alice traveled 120 km in 4 hours. What is the ratio of the average speed of John to average speed of Alice?

A. $4:3$ C. $6:4$

B. $3:4$ D. $5:3$

5) A ladder 10m long rests against a vertical wall. If the foot of the ladder is 6m away from the wall and the ladder just reaches the top of the wall, how high is the wall?

A. $10m$ C. $6m$

B. $8m$ D. $4m$

6) The low temperature in Anchorage, Alaska today was -4°F. The low temperature in Los Angeles, California was 63°F. What is the difference in the two low temperatures?

A. 59°   C. 57°

B. 67°   D. 14°

7) If 52% of a class are girls, and 30% of girls play tennis, what percent of the class play tennis?

A. 15.6%   C. 12.5%

B. 16.4%   D. 16%

8) The price of a car was $32,000 in 2014, $24,000 in 2015 and $18,000 in 2016. What is the rate of depreciation of the price of car per year?

A. 20%   C. 24%

B. 30%   D. 25%

9) A bag contains 6 red, 12 blue, 10 purple, and 4 orange marbles. One marble is selected at random. What is the probability that the marble chosen is blue?

A. $\frac{4}{13}$ C. $\frac{3}{16}$

B. $\frac{3}{8}$ D. $\frac{3}{5}$

10) The operator of an amusement park game kept track of how many tries it took participants to win the game. The following is the data from the first ten people:4,7,4,6,5,5,8,9,3,4. What is the median number of tries it took these participants to win the game?

A. 8   C. 4

B. 6   D. 5

This is the end of Session 1

Scientific Calculators are permitted for Session 2.

Time for Session 2: 60 Minutes

Session 2

11) Write 9.5×10^4 in decimal notation.

   A. 95,0000   C. 95,000

   B. 95,000   D. 0.00095

12) Jason and Bob are taking a $8\frac{3}{4}$ mile walk. If they walk at an average speed of $3\frac{1}{2}$ miles per hour, how long will it take them?

   A. $2\frac{2}{3}$ hours   C. $2\frac{1}{2}$ hours

   B. $30\frac{1}{8}$ hours   D. 5 hours

13) The width of a box is two third of its length. The height of the box is one fourth of its width. If the length of the box is 24 cm, what is the volume of the box?

   A. 1536   C. 1524

   B. 1546   D. 1527

14) If 45 % of A is 60 % of B, then B is what percent of A?

   A. 80%   C. 85%

   B. 133.33%   D. 125.5%

15) Mr. Reynolds owns $1\frac{3}{4}$ acres of land. He plans to buy the property next to his, which is $2\frac{3}{4}$ acres. How many acres will Mr. Reynolds own after the purchase?

   A. $5\frac{1}{4}$ C. $3\frac{1}{2}$

   B. $3\frac{3}{4}$ D. $4\frac{1}{2}$

16) In five successive hours, a car travels 25 km, 35 km, 30 km, 45 km and 50 km. In the next five hours, it travels with an average speed of 55 km per hour. Find the total distance the car traveled in 10 hours.

A. 475

C. 460

B. 490

D. 480

17) Where $\frac{3}{7} = \frac{x}{42}$, what is the value of x?

A. 21

C. 7

B. 6

D. 18

18) Rob purchased picnic food for $44.28 to share with three of his friends. They plan to split the cost evenly between the four friends. How much does each person need to pay Rob?

A. $8.05

C. $7.26

B. $8.30

D. $11.07

19) Hanna's sales goal for the week is $5,600. So far, she has sold $3,874.88 worth of merchandise. How much more does she need to sell to meet her goal?

A. $1,725.38

C. $2,574.38

B. $1,729.40

D. $1,725.12

20) What is the perimeter of a square in centimeters that has an area of 3969 cm²?

Write your answer in the box below. (don't write the measurement)

This is the end of Session 2

Scientific Calculators are permitted for Session 3.

Time for Session 3: 60 Minutes

Session 3

21) Find the area of a circle with a radius of 6 inches. The formula for the area of a circle is $A = \pi r^2$. Use 3.14 for π.

A. 37.68 square inches

C. 9.42 square inches

B. 113.04 square inches

D. 75.36 square inches

22) Mr. Carlos family are choosing a menu for their reception. They have 2 choices of appetizers, 6 choices of entrees, 3 choices of cake. How many different menu combinations are possible for them to choose?

A. 28

C. 38

B. 36

D. 34

23) The base side of a triangle is $2x + 1$ and height of that is $3x - 1$. What is the area of triangle?

A. $6x^2 + x - 1$

C. $3x^2 + x - 1$

B. $3x^2 + 0.5x - 0.5$

D. $6x^2 + 0.5x + 1$

24) 600 girls were surveyed about their favorite sport, 22% said that basketball is their favorite sport, 17% said that ice hockey is their favorite sport, and 35% said that softball is their favorite sport. The remaining girls said that field hockey is their favorite sport. How many of the girls surveyed said that field hockey is their favorite sport?

A. 150

C. 156

B. 155

D. 160

25) What is the value of x in the following system of equations?

$$\begin{cases} 3x - 6y = 0 \\ x + 3y = 4 \end{cases}$$

A. $\left(\frac{8}{5}, \frac{4}{5}\right)$

B. $\left(\frac{6}{5}, \frac{2}{5}\right)$

C. $(2,3)$

D. $\left(-\frac{8}{5}, -\frac{6}{5}\right)$

26) The diagonal of a rectangle is 15 inches long and the height of the rectangle is 12 inches. What is the perimeter of the rectangle in inches?

A. 40

B. 44

C. 42

D. 45

27) The ratio of boys and girls in a class is $6:8$. If there are 70 students in the class, how many more boys should be enrolled to make the ratio $1:1$?

A. 12

B. 10

C. 14

D. 8

28) Simplify $3x^3y^2z(2x^2yz)^3 =$

A. $6x^9y^5z^4$

B. $24x^9y^5z^4$

C. $12x^9y^5z^2$

D. $6x^8y^5z^4$

29) The square of a number is $\frac{81}{144}$. What is the cube of that number?

A. $\frac{512}{1728}$

B. $\frac{343}{1728}$

C. $\frac{729}{1728}$

D. $\frac{729}{1331}$

30) Nine minus five times a number, x, is no less than 39. Which of the following expressions represents all the possible values of the number?

A. $x \leq 6$

B. $x \geq -6$

C. $x \leq -6$

D. $x \geq 6$

This is the end of Session 3

This is the End of Practice Test 2.   STOP

FSA Practice Tests Answers and Explanations

FSA Math Practice Test 1				FSA Math Practice Test 2			
1	C	21	C	1	A	21	B
2	$5\frac{7}{10}$	22	D	2	D	22	B
3	D	23	D	3	C	23	B
4	-37	24	D	4	A	24	C
5	768	25	A	5	B	25	A
6	C	26	D	6	B	26	C
7	D	27	C	7	A	27	B
8	C	28	B	8	D	28	B
9	60	29	B	9	B	29	C
10	C	30	C	10	D	30	C
11	B			11	B		
12	D			12	C		
13	D			13	A		
14	C			14	B		
15	B			15	D		
16	B			16	C		
17	D			17	D		
18	B			18	D		
19	D			19	D		
20	C			20	252		

FSA Math Practice Test 1 Explanations

1) Choice C is correct

Jason ate $\frac{1}{2}$ of 8 parts of his pizza. It means 4 parts out of 8 parts ($\frac{1}{2}$ of 8 parts is $x \Rightarrow x = 4$) and left 4 parts. Eva ate $\frac{3}{4}$ of 8 parts of her pizza. It means 6 parts out of 8 parts ($\frac{3}{4}$ of 8 parts is $x \Rightarrow x = 6$) and left 2 parts.

Therefore, they ate $(4 + 6)$ parts out of $(8 + 8)$ parts of their pizza and left $(4 + 2)$ parts out of $(8 + 8)$ parts of their pizza that equals to: $\frac{6}{16}$

After simplification, the answer is: $\frac{3}{8}$

2) The answer is $5\frac{7}{10}$ miles.

Robert runs $3\frac{1}{10}$ miles on Saturday and $2 \times (3\frac{1}{10})$ miles on Monday and Wednesday. Robert wants to run a total of 18 miles this week.

Therefore: $3\frac{1}{10} + 2 \times (3\frac{1}{10})$ should be subtracted from 18:

$18 - \left(3\frac{1}{10} + 2\left(3\frac{1}{10}\right)\right) = 15 - 9\frac{3}{10} = 5\frac{7}{10}$ miles.

3) Choice A is correct

Let x be the integer. Then: $2x + 20 = 68$. Subtract 20 both sides: $2x = 48$. Divide both sides by $2 \Rightarrow x = 24$

4) The answer is: –37

Use PEMDAS (order of operation):

$[3 \times (-21) + (5 \times 2)] - (-25) + [(-3) \times 6] \div 2 = [-63 + 10] + 25 + [-18] \div 2$
$$= -53 + 25 - 9 = -37$$

5) The answer is 768 cm.

Write the proportion and solve for missing side.

$\frac{\text{Smaller triangle height}}{\text{Smaller triangle base}} = \frac{\text{Bigger triangle height}}{\text{Bigger triangle base}} \Rightarrow \frac{100cm}{160cm} = \frac{100+380cm}{x} \Rightarrow x = 768cm$

6) Choice C is correct.

Write the proportion and solve. $\frac{3ft}{2ft} = \frac{x}{38ft} \Rightarrow x = 57\ ft$

7) Choice D is correct.

The distance that Mike runs can be found by the following equation:

$D_M = 5.5t + 7.5$. The distance Julia runs can be found by $D_J = 8t$

Julia catches Mike if they run the same distance. Therefore:

$8t = 5.5t + 7.5 \Rightarrow 2.5t = 7.5 \Rightarrow t = \frac{7.5}{2.5} = 3\ hours$

8) Choice C is correct

x is the number of all sales profit and 2% of it is:

$2\% \times x = 0.02x$. Employer's revenue: $0.2x + 7,000$

9) The answer is 60.

Jason needs an 75% average to pass the exams. Therefore, the sum of 5 exams must be at least $5 \times 75 = 375$. The sum of 4 exams is: $68 + 72 + 85 + 90 = 315$. The minimum score Jason can earn on final test to pass is: $375 - 315 = 60$

10) Choice C is correct.

We can write: $\frac{25}{100} = \frac{8}{x} \Rightarrow \frac{8 \times 100}{25} = x \Rightarrow x = 32$

11) Choice B is correct.

Let x be the amount of angle and y be the amount of its supplement. The angle and its supplement are $180°$ in total ($x + y = 180°$). we have: $x = \frac{1}{5}y$

$x + y = \frac{1}{5}y + y = 180° \Rightarrow y = 150°$ and $x = 30°$

12) Choice D is correct

$y = x + 1 \Rightarrow$ if $x = 0$ therefore $y = 1$ and if $y = 0$ therefore $x = -1$. Hence answer d is correct.

13) Choice D is correct

$\begin{cases} \frac{-x}{2} + \frac{y}{4} = 1 \\ \frac{-5y}{6} + 2x = 4 \end{cases} \Rightarrow$ Multiply the top equation by 4. Then,

$\begin{cases} -2x + y = 4 \\ \frac{-5y}{6} + 2x = 4 \end{cases} \Rightarrow$ Add two equations.

$\frac{1}{6}y = 8 \Rightarrow y = 48$, plug in the value of y into the first equation $\Rightarrow x = 22$

14) Choice C is correct

$\begin{cases} x + 4y = 10 \\ 5x + 10y = 20 \end{cases} \Rightarrow$ Multiply the top equation by -5 then,

$\begin{cases} -5x - 20y = -50 \\ 5x + 10y = 20 \end{cases} \Rightarrow$ Add two equations

$-10y = -30 \rightarrow y = 3$, plug in the value of y into the first equation

$x + 4y = 10 \Rightarrow x + 4(3) = 10 \Rightarrow x + 12 = 10$

Subtract 12 from both sides of the equation. Then: $x + 12 = 10 \rightarrow x = -2$

15) Choice B is correct.

$\frac{21 + 18 + 16 + x}{4} = 20 \Rightarrow \frac{55 + x}{4} = 20 \Rightarrow 55 + x = 80 \Rightarrow x = 25$

16) Choice B is correct.

Solve for x. $5 \le 3x - 1 < 11 \Rightarrow$ (add 1 all sides)

$5 + 1 \le 3x - 1 + 1 < 11 + 1 \Rightarrow 6 \le 3x < 12 \Rightarrow$ (divide all sides by 3)

$2 \le x < 4 \Rightarrow x$ is between 2 and 4.

17) Choice D is correct.

Distance between two points is equal: $\sqrt{(x_1 - x_2)^2 + (y_1 - y_2)^2}$

18) Choice B is correct

Distance between two points is equal: $\sqrt{(x_1 - x_2)^2 + (y_1 - y_2)^2}$

$\sqrt{(9-4)^2 + (7-(-5))^2} = \sqrt{(5)^2 + (12)^2} = \sqrt{169} = 13$

19) Choice D is correct

The slop of line A is: $m = \frac{y_2 - y_1}{x_2 - x_1} = \frac{-10-8}{4-(-8)} = -\frac{3}{2}$

Also $(y - y_1) = m(x - x_1) \Rightarrow y - 8 = -\frac{3}{2}(x + 8) \Rightarrow y = -\frac{3}{2}x - 4$

20) Choice C is correct

The value of y in the x-intercept of a line is zero. Then:

$y = 0 \to 10x - 4(0) = 5 \to 10x = 5 \to x = \frac{1}{2}$. Then, x-intercept of the line is $\frac{1}{2}$

21) Choice C is correct

The total amount of money Giselle made as a carpenter can be modeled by $20x$, and the total amount of money she made as a blacksmith can be modeled by $25y$. Since these together add up to \$690, we get the following equation:

$20x + 25y = 690$.

We are also given that last week, Giselle worked as a carpenter and a blacksmith for a total of 30 hours. This can be expressed as: $x + y = 30 \Rightarrow y = 30 - x$

Therefor $20x + 25(30 - x) = 690 \Rightarrow x = 12 \ and \ y = 18$

22) Choice D is correct

$\begin{cases} 3x + y = 8 \\ -5x - 2y = 0 \end{cases} \Rightarrow$ Multiply the top equation by 2 then,

$\begin{cases} 6x + 2y = 16 \\ -5x - 2y = 0 \end{cases} \Rightarrow$ Add two equations

$x = 16$, plug in the value of y into the first equation

$3x + y = 8 \to 3(16) + y = 8 \to y = -40$

23) Choice D is correct

Let $x =$ the total miles of the ride.

Therefore, $x - 1 = $ the additional miles of the ride. The correct equation takes \$1.25 and adds it to \$1.15 times the number of additional miles, $x - 1$. Translating, this becomes: $y(the \ total \ cost) = 1.25 + 1.15(x - 1)$, which is the same equation as $y = 1.15(x - 1) + 1.25$.

24) Choice D is correct.

Write as two points in terms of: (number of people, cost in\$) (15,120) and (25,200). Find the equation of the line using: $m = \frac{y2-y1}{x2-x1}$ and $y = mx + b$

Equation: $Y = 8x$ plug in $x = 40$, $y = 8(40) = 320$. A party of 40 people will cost \$320.00.

25) Choice A is correct

$C = 250 + 150h$. Assuming the initial meeting counts for the 1st hour, you would plug in $h = 25$ for a total cost of $4000.00.

26) Choice D is correct

Let the number be x. Then the other number= $x + 8$. Sum of two numbers= 30. According to question, $x + x + 8 = 30 \Rightarrow 2x + 8 = 30 \Rightarrow 2x = 22 \Rightarrow x = 11$. Therefore, $x + 8 = 11 + 8 = 19$

27) Choice C is correct.

$$0.0000005823 = 5.823 \times 10^{-7}$$

28) Choice B is correct.

$$28,000,000,000 = 2.8 \times 10^{10}$$

29) Choice B is correct.

The area of greater circle is: $A_g = \pi r^2 = \pi . (45)^2 = 6361.7mm^2$

The area of smaller circle is: $A_s = \pi r^2 = \pi . (33)^2 = 3421.2mm^2$

Then area of colored part is $A_c = A_g - A_s = 6361.7 - 3421.2 = 2940.5mm^2$

30) Choice C is correct.

When a point is reflected over y axes, the (x) coordinate of that point changes to $(-x)$, while its y coordinate remains the same.

FSA Practice Test 2 Explanations

1) Choice A is correct.

Since $m = 5$ and $(0, -7)$ is the y-intercept, $b = -7$, then substituting into the form $y = mx + b$ will give us the equation of the line: $y = 5x - 7$

2) Choice D is correct.

To find the discount, multiply the number by $(100\% - rate\ of\ discount)$.

Therefore, for the first discount we get:

$(350)(100\% - 15\%) = (350)(0.85)$

For the next 10 % discount: $(350)(0.85)(0.90)$

3) Choice C is correct.

Let x be the number. Write the equation and solve for x. $(32 - x) \div x = 7$

Multiply both sides by x. $(32 - x) = 7x$, then add x both sides. $32 = 8x$, now divide both sides by 8. $x = 4$

4) Choice A is correct.

The average speed of john is: $240 \div 6 = 40$ km

The average speed of Alice is: $120 \div 4 = 30$ km

Write the ratio and simplify. $40:30 \Rightarrow 4:3$

5) Choice B is correct.

Let AC be the ladder. Therefore, $AC = 10m$
Let BC be the distance between the foot of the ladder and the wall.
Therefore, $BC = 6m$, $\triangle ABC$ forms a right-angled triangle, right angled at B.
By Pythagoras theorem, $AC^2 = AB^2 + BC^2 \Rightarrow 102 = AB^2 + 62$ Or
$AB^2 = 102 - 62 = 100 - 36 = 64$ Or $AB = \sqrt{64} = 8m$. Hence, the wall is $8m$ high.

6) Choice B is correct.

Visualize a number line. The distance from (-4) to 0 is 4. Then, the distance from 0 to 63 is 63. Add the two distances together to get 67. $63 + 4 = 67$.

7) Choice A is correct.

The percent of girls playing tennis is: $52\% \times 30\% = 0.52 \times 0.30 = 0.156 = 15.6\%$

8) Choice D is correct.

Use this formula: Percent of Change: $\frac{New\ Value - Old\ Value}{Old\ Value} \times 100\%$

$\frac{24000 - 32000}{32000} \times 100\% = 25\%$ and $\frac{18000 - 24000}{24000} \times 100\% = 25\%$

9) Choice B is correct.

The probability of blue is $\frac{blue}{total}$. The number of blue marbles is 12, and the total number of marbles is 16 $(6 + 12 + 10 + 4 = 32)$. Therefore, the probability of choosing a blue is $\frac{12}{32} = \frac{3}{8}$

10) Choice D is correct.

First, put the numbers in order from least to greatest, and then find the middle of the set. 4,7,4,6,5,5,8,9,3,4. The middle is the average (mean) of the 5th and 6th data items. The mean of 5 and 5 is 5.

11) Choice B is correct.

Move the decimal point 4 places to the right to get 95,000.

12) Choice C is correct.

To find the amount of time that it took Jason and Bob, divide the distance $8\frac{3}{4}$ by the rate $3\frac{1}{2}$. $8\frac{3}{4} \div 3\frac{1}{2} = \frac{35}{4} \div \frac{7}{2} = \frac{35}{4} \times \frac{2}{7} = 2\frac{1}{2}$

13) Choice A is correct.

If the length of the box is 24, then the width of the box is two third of it, 16, and the height of the box is 4 (one fourth of the width). The volume of the box is: $V = lwh$ = $(24)(16)(4) = 1536$

14) Choice B is correct.

Write the equation and solve for B: $0.45A = 0.60B$, divide both sides by 0.60, then: $\frac{0.45\,A}{0.60} = B$, therefore: $B = 0.75\,A$, and B is 0.75 times of A or it's 133.33% of A.

15) Choice D is correct.

Add the two pieces of land together; $1\frac{3}{4} + 2\frac{3}{4} = 3\frac{3}{4}$. Add the whole numbers. Since the denominators are already the same, just add the numerators and keep the denominator the same; $\frac{6}{4}$ can be simplified to $1\frac{1}{2}$. Add this to the whole number to get $4\frac{1}{2}$ acres.

16) Choice C is correct.

Add the first 5 numbers. $25 + 35 + 30 + 45 + 50 = 185$

To find the distance traveled in the next 5 hours, multiply the average by number of hours. $Distance = Average \times Rate = 55 \times 5 = 275$, Add both numbers. $275 + 185 = 460$

17) Choice D is correct.

Determine what number 7 was multiplied by to get 42 and multiply the numerator by the same number. Seven was multiplied by six, so $3 \times 6 = 18$. The value of x is 18.

18) Choice D is correct.

You must divide the cost of the food by 4 to split the cost evenly among the four friends; $\$44.28 \div 4 = \$11.07$.

19) Choice D is correct.

You must find the difference (subtraction) between her goal and what she has already sold. Add a decimal and two zeros to the end of $\$5,600$ ($\$5,600.00$) to make the subtraction easier; $\$5,600.00 - \$3,874.88 = \$1,725.12$.

20) Answer is 252.

The area of the square is 3969. Therefore, the side of the square is square root of the area. $\sqrt{3969} = 63$. Four times the side of the square is the perimeter: $4 \times 63 = 252$

21) Choice B is correct.

Substitute 6 for r in the formula $A = \pi r^2$. $A = 3.14 \times 6^2 = 113.04$

22) Choice B is correct.

To find the number of possible outfit combinations, multiply number of options for each factor: $2 \times 6 \times 3 = 36$

23) Choice B is correct.

Area of triangle is: $\frac{b \times h}{2} \Rightarrow \frac{1}{2}(2x + 1)(3x - 1) = \frac{1}{2}(6x^2 + x - 1) \Rightarrow$

$$A = 3x^2 + 0.5x - 0.5$$

24) Choice B is correct.

The percent must add up to 100%; $22\% + 17\% + 35\% = 74\%$. If 74% of the girls surveyed have been accounted for, the remainder of the girls must have said that field hockey is their favorite sport. To find the percent that said field hockey is their favorite sport, subtract 74% from 100%; $100\% - 74\% = 26\%$; The girls said that field hockey is their favorite sport is $0.26 \times 600 = 156$

25) Choice A is correct.

$\begin{matrix} 3x - 6y = 0 \\ x + 3y = 4 \end{matrix}$. Multiply the second equation by 2. then add it to the first equation.

$2(x + 3y = 4) \Rightarrow 2x + 6y = 8 \Rightarrow \genfrac{}{}{1pt}{}{\begin{matrix}3x-6y=0\\ +2x+6y=8\end{matrix}}{5x=8} \Rightarrow x = \frac{8}{5}$. $3x - 6y = 0 \Rightarrow$

$\frac{24}{5} - 6y = 0 \Rightarrow 6y = \frac{24}{5} \Rightarrow y = \frac{4}{5}$

26) Choice C is correct.

Let x be the width of the rectangle. Use Pythagorean Theorem:

$a^2 + b^2 = c^2$

$x^2 + 12^2 = 15^2 \Rightarrow x^2 + 144 = 225 \Rightarrow x^2 = 225 - 144 = 81 \Rightarrow x = 9$

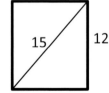

Perimeter of the rectangle $= 2(length + width) = 2(12 + 9) = 2\ (21) = 42$

27) Choice B is correct.

The ratio of boy to girls is 6:8. Therefore, there are 6 boys out of 14 students. To find the answer, first divide the total number of students by 14, then multiply the result by 6. $70 \div 14 = 5 \Rightarrow 5 \times 6 = 30$

There are 30 boys and 40(70–30) girls. So, 10 more boys should be enrolled to make the ratio 1:1

28) Choice B is correct.
29) Choice C is correct.

The square of a number is $\frac{81}{144}$, then the number is the square root of $\frac{81}{144}$

$\sqrt{\frac{81}{144}} = \frac{9}{12}$. The cube of the number is: $(\frac{9}{12})^3 = \frac{729}{1728}$

30) Choice C is correct.

www.EffortlessMath.com

… So Much More Online!

✓ FREE Math lessons

✓ More Math learning books!

✓ Mathematics Worksheets

———————

✓ Online Math Tutors

Need a PDF version of this book?

Send email to: info@EffortlessMath.com